Slavery, Equality, and the American Revolution

This book is the fifth in a series in AEI's
"We Hold These Truths: America at 250" initiative.

WE HOLD THESE TRUTHS: AMERICA AT 250

Democracy and the American Revolution

Capitalism and the American Revolution

Religion and the American Revolution

*Natural Rights, the Common Good,
and the American Revolution*

Slavery, Equality, and the American Revolution

WE HOLD THESE TRUTHS

★ ★ ★

AMERICA AT
— 250 —

Slavery, Equality, and the American Revolution

Edited by Yuval Levin,
Adam J. White, and John Yoo

AEI PRESS

Publisher for the American Enterprise Institute
WASHINGTON, DC

ISBN-13: 978-0-8447-5106-1 (Paperback)

Library of Congress Cataloging in Publication data have been applied for.

A≡I PRESS

Publisher for the American Enterprise Institute
for Public Policy Research
1789 Massachusetts Avenue, NW
Washington, DC 20036
www.aei.org

Printed in the United States of America

Contents

Introduction

YUVAL LEVIN

July 4, 2026, marks the 250th anniversary of the Declaration of Independence and, therefore, of the United States of America. Such an anniversary is a time for celebration, and Americans will certainly mark it with great fanfare. But celebrations of our nation's founding and its history are now always unavoidably accompanied by accusations that the founding generation ignored or promoted the evils of slavery and that the Declaration's assertions about the truths of human equality and liberty could not have been the honest views of slaveholders.

Our generation is hardly the first to argue that slavery casts a shadow over the claims of the founding. That has been the view of many Americans from the very beginning. Indeed, Thomas Jefferson himself, in his original draft of the Declaration of Independence, included among the colonial grievances against King George III the accusation that the king had abided the violation of the basic rights of "persons of a distant people, who never offended him, captivating and carrying them into slavery in another hemisphere," and had "determined to keep open a market where men should be bought & sold."[1] But the Second Continental Congress struck those lines from the final document.

In a sense, this back-and-forth contained the seeds of the moral quandary that still confronts us over slavery and the founding. Jefferson was himself a slave owner and so a participant in the very market he denounced. How could his denunciations be squared with his actions? And what can we make of the congress's refusal to take up the question of slavery one way or another?

1

Such questions remained unanswered, and they festered and grew in the decades that followed as slavery metastasized into an intensely malignant sickness in the American body politic. The horrid practice became entrenched in the South, and the hypocrisy of its persistence in a nation that never ceased to declare itself a cradle of liberty came to seem increasingly untenable. For some, this was a reason to dismiss the Declaration and its claims. For others, those very claims were a reason to reject slavery and seek its end in America. Abraham Lincoln understood that the nation faced a choice between these two alternatives, and he framed the Civil War in just those terms, putting the Declaration at the very core of the American story.

Lincoln acknowledged that some of the signers of the Declaration, and indeed its lead author, did not live up to its claims about human equality. But those claims have had a power of their own, which those signers and authors intended. Those founders, Lincoln said,

> meant to set up a standard maxim for free society, which should be familiar to all, and revered by all; constantly looked to, constantly labored for, and even though never perfectly attained, constantly approximated, and thereby constantly spreading and deepening its influence, and augmenting the happiness and value of life to all people of all colors everywhere.[2]

This remains an unequaled description of the peculiar power of the Declaration of Independence, from its day right through to ours.

But the argument that the very fact of slavery made hypocrites of the founders and proved that they never meant what they said in declaring independence has remained with us nonetheless. It is an argument made anew in every generation and that must be taken seriously and contended with. The questions it raises challenge us to sharpen our understanding of the character of our country and speak as much to its future as to its past.

Better understanding the character of our society this way is precisely the purpose of the American Enterprise Institute's "We Hold These Truths: America at 250" initiative, an ambitious celebration of the founding of which this volume forms a part. Over several years leading up to the anniversary of the Declaration of Independence, we are inviting scholars both within AEI and from other institutions to take up a series of themes important to understanding the American Revolution. These scholars represent a variety of fields and viewpoints, so they approach each of these themes from various angles. The papers they produce are being published in a series of edited volumes intended to help Americans think more deeply and clearly about our nation's origins, character, and prospects.

Slavery, Equality, and the American Revolution is the fifth of those books. Its chapters began as papers presented at an AEI conference held in Washington, DC, on February 10, 2025. Other volumes in the series consider the American Revolution in relation to other themes, such as democracy, religion, natural rights, and the Constitution. In each case, our goal is to help reintroduce readers to their nation's history, thereby enabling them to maturely appreciate the reasons for celebrating the extraordinary milestone of its 250th anniversary.

In the chapters that follow, five eminent scholars of history, philosophy, law, and government consider how we ought to understand slavery's place in the American story and what we should make of the tension between the truths asserted in the Declaration and the practice of that wicked institution in the nation that declared itself committed to those truths.

Randy E. Barnett argues that the authors of both the Declaration and the Constitution meant what they said and that what they said was that all men are created equal and therefore that slavery was unjust.

Kurt T. Lash shows that federalism and freedom have been intertwined ideals from the beginning and that freedom of action for the states in the early republic was not a tool for the defenders of slavery but an essential instrument for the cause of abolition.

Lucas E. Morel traces Abraham Lincoln's case for the centrality of the Declaration in any conception of the American character and therefore for the consistency of an antislavery defense of the founding.

Justin Driver considers Frederick Douglass's critiques of the founding and illuminates how generations of Americans have drawn on the

Declaration to address the deepest moral challenges to the legitimacy of the American republic.

And Diana Schaub follows the evolution of Douglass's own conception of the founding, which traces a path that she suggests today's skeptical students would be wise to consider and follow.

The scope of these arguments helps show just how serious a moral challenge the practice of slavery posed to the American founding and just how deep are the moral roots of the founders' core commitments. Two hundred fifty years after the Declaration set up its standard maxim for a free society, its influence still spreads and deepens.

Notes

1. *The Papers of Thomas Jefferson*, ed. Julian P. Boyd, vol. 1, *1760–1776* (Princeton University Press, 1950), 246–47.

2. Abraham Lincoln, "Speech at Springfield, Illinois," June 26, 1857, in *The Collected Works of Abraham Lincoln*, ed. Roy P. Basler, vol. 2, *1848–1858* (Rutgers University Press, 1953), 406.

1

But What About Slavery?

RANDY E. BARNETT

The United States was not founded in 1789, and the Constitution is not our founding document. The United States was founded in 1776, and our founding document is the Declaration of Independence that Congress unanimously adopted. The Declaration officially announced the American theory of government, which can be summarized as "first come rights; and then comes government."[1] Specifically, the Declaration affirmed the individual, natural, and inalienable rights to life, liberty, and the pursuit of happiness. It then affirmed that "to secure these rights, Governments are instituted among Men, deriving their just powers from the consent of the governed."

To this, today's vocal critics of the United States—both its founding and its Constitution—immediately reply, "But what about slavery?"[2] Unknowingly, and sometimes knowingly, these critics are accepting as accurate Chief Justice Roger Taney's characterization of the Declaration and his interpretation of the Constitution in the notorious 1857 Supreme Court decision *Dred Scott v. Sandford*.

Dred Scott denied that black Americans could claim the constitutional protections that citizenship afforded. Writing for the majority, Taney infamously asserted that the Declaration's ringing affirmation of equal natural rights to life, liberty, and the pursuit of happiness did not apply to *all* men at the time it was written:

> It is difficult at this day to realize the state of public opinion in relation to that unfortunate race, which prevailed in the civilized and enlightened portions of the world at the time of the

Declaration of Independence, and when the Constitution of the United States was framed and adopted.[3]

What was this public opinion about persons of African descent? According to Taney,

> They had for more than a century before been regarded as beings of an inferior order, and altogether unfit to associate with the white race, either in social or political relations; and so far inferior, that *they had no rights which the white man was bound to respect*; and that the negro might justly and lawfully be reduced to slavery for his benefit.[4] (Emphasis added.)

Are today's critics of the American founding right to adopt Taney's reading of the Declaration and the Constitution? I think they are decidedly wrong.

Public meaning originalism claims that the meaning of the Constitution is the meaning it had at the time of its adoption or amendment, whether in 1789, when the Constitution was ratified, or in 1868, when the 14th Amendment was passed.[5] In this chapter, I begin by identifying the original public meaning of the Declaration of Independence. In so doing, I reframe the founding from how critics have mischaracterized it. I then turn to the original public meaning of the Constitution to consider how consistent it was with the principles the Declaration affirmed.

None of the facts on which I rely are contested by historians, but some have been downplayed or largely forgotten. Proper attention to these neglected facts will counter the negative spin that has been put on the founding and the Constitution. Despite the failure to abolish slavery in 1776, studying the original public meaning of the Declaration and its relationship to the Constitution shows that when it comes to the founding, Americans today still have much to be proud of.

Chief Justice Taney's Interpretation of the Declaration

On their face, the Declaration's words seem completely hostile to the institution of slavery. So, like today's critics of our founding, it was necessary for Taney to explain them away. In his opinion for the Court in *Dred Scott*, Taney admitted that the "general words" of the Declaration "would seem to embrace the whole human family, and if they were used in a similar instrument at this day would be so understood."[6] In other words, Taney affirmed that by 1857, the public meaning of the Declaration's words was inimical to slavery.

Attributing the public meaning of the Declaration's words in 1857 to the Declaration's meaning in 1776, Taney contended, would be to misinterpret its original meaning as the founders understood it. In 1776, he wrote, "it is too clear for dispute, that the enslaved African race were not intended to be included, and formed no part of the people who framed and adopted this declaration." This was because "if the language, as understood in that day," had included enslaved persons, "the conduct of the distinguished *men who framed* the Declaration of Independence would have been utterly and flagrantly inconsistent with the principles they asserted."[7] (Emphasis added.)

In short, Taney admitted that the Declaration's words were flagrantly inconsistent with the institution of slavery. The only way to render the Declaration consistent with slavery was to appeal to its drafters' original intentions.[8] In this way, Taney's proslavery reading of the Constitution in *Dred Scott* started with claiming a proslavery reading of the Declaration—a reading the two dissenting justices in *Dred Scott* vehemently disputed.

The issue in *Dred Scott* did not concern the citizenship of enslaved blacks. It concerned whether free blacks could ever be United States citizens. Taney's analysis of the founding was designed to support his opinion that persons of African descent, regardless of whether they were free or even whether they were deemed by a state to be a citizen, could never be a "citizen" *of the United States* and entitled to the fundamental privileges and immunities that such citizenship entailed:

> After such an uniform course of legislation as we have stated, by the colonies, by the States, and by Congress, running through a period of more than a century, it would seem that to call persons thus marked and stigmatized, "citizens" of the United States, "fellow-citizens," a constituent part of the sovereignty, would be an abuse of terms.[9]

In sharp contrast, the two dissenting justices, John McLean and Benjamin Curtis, claimed that, while enslaved blacks were undeniably excluded from the polity at the founding, free blacks were considered a part of "the people" who established the Constitution. McLean wrote, "I admit the Government was not made especially for the colored race, yet many of them were citizens of the New England States, and exercised, the rights of suffrage when the Constitution was adopted."[10]

Curtis added more details:

> An argument from speculative premises, however well chosen, that the then state of opinion in the Commonwealth of Massachusetts was not consistent with the natural rights of people of color who were born on that soil, and that they were not, by the Constitution of 1780 of that State, admitted to the condition of citizens, would be received with surprise by the people of that State who know their own political history. It is true, beyond all controversy that persons of color, descended from African slaves, were by that Constitution made citizens of the State, and such of them as have had the necessary qualifications have held and exercised the elective franchise, as citizens, from that time to the present.[11]

Curtis then quoted from several state constitutions. In New Hampshire, the right to vote was conferred on "'every inhabitant of the State having the necessary qualifications,' of which color or descent was not one." New York "gave the right to vote to 'every male inhabitant, who shall have resided,' &c., making no discrimination between free colored persons and others." In New Jersey, the right to vote extended to "all inhabitants of this colony, of full age, who are worth £50 proclamation money, clear estate."[12]

It was true, he admitted, that sometime after the founding, some Northern states imposed racial restrictions on voting, as Taney had alleged. However, Curtis contended,

> these changes can have no other effect upon the present inquiry, except to show, that before they were made, no such restrictions existed, and colored in common with white persons, were not only citizens of those States, but entitled to the elective franchise on the same qualifications as white persons, as they now are in New Hampshire and Massachusetts.[13]

Curtis then turned his attention to Taney's claim that those who drafted the Declaration would have been hypocrites had they intended its abstract principles to apply to persons of African descent:

> My own opinion is, that a calm comparison of these assertions of universal abstract truths, and of their own individual opinions and acts, would not leave these men under any reproach of inconsistency; that the great truths they asserted on that solemn occasion, they were ready and anxious to make effectual, wherever a necessary regard to circumstances, which no statesman can disregard without producing more evil than good, would allow; and that it would not be just to them, nor true in itself, to allege that they intended to say that the Creator of all men had endowed the white race, exclusively, with the great natural rights which the Declaration of Independence asserts. But this is not the place to vindicate their memory.[14]

All that needed to be demonstrated for purposes of the case was that written state constitutions and political practice "show, in a manner which no argument can obscure, that, in some of the original thirteen States, free colored persons, before and at the time of the formation of the Constitution, were citizens of those States."[15]

It is worth highlighting that two justices of the Supreme Court contested Taney's historiography on the spot. Noting this avoids the charge that we are anachronistically superimposing our judgment of Taney's erroneous interpretation of the revolutionary period onto 19th-century society by showing that in 1857, not everyone shared Taney's understanding of the founding. Likewise, the facts McLean and Curtis related undermine the claim that we are similarly imposing a modern and color-blind interpretation of rights onto the founding itself.

McLean and Curtis's view of the Declaration and founding has been borne out by respected historians of today. To see why, let's begin with how the "abstract truths" in the Declaration came to be there.

Drafting the Declaration

On June 11, 1776, the Continental Congress appointed a committee to draft a declaration to effectuate Richard Henry Lee's motion

> that these United Colonies are, and of right ought to be, free and independent states; that they are absolved from all allegiance to the British Crown: and that all political connexion between them and the state of Great Britain is, and ought to be, totally dissolved.[16]

This was the legal purpose of the Declaration. In addition, as John Hancock later put it, such a declaration would provide "the Ground & Foundation of a future Government."[17]

The Committee of Five consisted of the senior Pennsylvanian Benjamin Franklin, Roger Sherman of Connecticut, New York's Robert Livingston, Massachusetts's stalwart champion of independence John Adams, and a rather quiet 33-year-old Virginian named Thomas Jefferson. After a series of meetings to decide on the outline of the Declaration, the committee assigned Jefferson to write the first draft.[18]

Jefferson did not have much time. With no executive, the war was being run entirely by congressional committees, and the business of waging war pressed heavily on its members. Over a six-month period, Jefferson served on some 34 different committees, which kept him very busy. On June 17, for example, the committee overseeing the Canadian campaign submitted two reports to Congress, both in Jefferson's own hand. Two members of the Virginia delegation had left Philadelphia, increasing the pressure on Jefferson to attend the sessions of Congress.[19]

So, with the press of other matters, Jefferson did not have three leisurely weeks to write. He had merely a few days. Needing to work fast, he had to borrow. Historian Pauline Maier tells us that Jefferson had two sources in front of him from which to crib. The first was a list of grievances in his draft preamble for the Virginia constitution—a list that was strikingly similar to the first group of charges against the king that ended up in the Declaration. The second was a preliminary version of the Virginia Declaration of Rights that George Mason had drafted in his room at the Raleigh Tavern in Williamsburg, the city where Virginia's provincial convention was being held concurrently.[20]

Mason's May 27 draft proved handy indeed in composing the Declaration's famous preamble. Its first two articles present two fundamental ideas. The first idea is that *first come rights and then comes government*. Here is how Mason expressed it:

> That all men are born equally free and independant, and have certain inherent natural rights, of which they cannot, by any compact, deprive or divest their posterity; among which are, the enjoyment of life and liberty, with the means of acquiring

and possessing property, and pursuing and obtaining happiness and safety.[21]

So, in Mason's draft, not only do all persons have "certain . . . natural rights" of life, liberty, and property, but these rights cannot be taken away "by any compact." These inherent individual natural rights, of which the people cannot divest their posterity, are therefore retained by them. Mason's words would become even more canonical than Jefferson's more succinct version in the Declaration of Independence, as variations were incorporated into several state constitutions. Later, James Madison proposed they be added to the preamble of the Constitution by way of an amendment. That did not happen, but Mason's description of retained rights would be echoed in the Ninth Amendment and, much later, in the privileges or immunities clause of the 14th Amendment.

Article 2 of Mason's draft then identified the persons who compose a government as the *servants* of the sovereign people, rather than their masters: "That all power is vested in, and consequently derived from the people; that magistrates are their trustees *and servants*, and at all times amenable to them."[22] (Emphasis added.) As trustees and servants, those people who serve as governing magistrates are to respect the inherent natural rights retained by the people.

Jefferson then compressed all this into 55 compelling words:

> We hold these truths to be self-evident, that all men are created equal, that they are endowed by their Creator with certain unalienable Rights, that among these are Life, Liberty and the pursuit of Happiness.—That to secure these rights, Governments are instituted among Men, deriving their just powers from the consent of the governed.

Adams later recalled that Jefferson took only a day or two to write the first draft, which was then turned over to the committee for its feedback before it was submitted to Congress. Although this draft was then heavily edited and shortened by Congress sitting as a committee of the whole, its preamble was left pretty much as Jefferson had submitted it.

The developments that followed undercut the claim by Taney and today's critics that the Declaration of Independence did not mean what it said.

The Declaration's Antislavery Implications

Taney's history of the founding, like the history propounded by those who today criticize the Constitution, is deeply misleading. For a start, the institution of chattel slavery was as old as mankind, prevalent worldwide, and by no means limited to the enslavement of African people. In 1776, the United States was on the leading edge of the modern movement to abolish chattel slavery.

As Princeton University historian Sean Wilentz has noted in his important book *No Property in Man: Slavery and Antislavery at the Nation's Founding*, "In 1775, five days before the battles of Lexington and Concord, ten Philadelphians, seven of them Quakers, founded the first antislavery society in world history, the Society for the Relief of Free Negroes Unlawfully Held in Bondage."[23] This group was later reorganized as the Pennsylvania Society for Promoting the Abolition of Slavery.

In January 1777, just five months after the signing of the Declaration, the Vermont Republic was founded as an independent state. By declaring that "all men are born equally free and independent,"[24] its constitution became the first constitution in human history to abolish slavery.[25] But Vermont did not invent this language. It was borrowed from Mason's draft of the Virginia Declaration of Rights, quoted above. Massachusetts also included Mason's language in its constitution. In three cases decided between 1781 and 1783, four years before the United States Constitution was drafted, the Massachusetts high court relied on this language to hold chattel slavery unconstitutional in that state.

This timeline is important. In 1776, when the United States was founded, the legal institution of slavery existed in every state in the union.

But by 1787, when the Constitution was being written in Philadelphia, five of these states—Connecticut, Massachusetts, New Hampshire, Pennsylvania, and Rhode Island—had abolished or begun to abolish slavery. Then, in 1791, Vermont became the 14th state of the union, bringing the count of free states to six. In 1799, New York began the process of emancipation by enacting a gradual abolition law. Five years later, New Jersey followed with its own gradual emancipation law.

During the same summer that the Philadelphia convention was deliberating over a new constitution, in New York, the Congress formed under the Articles of Confederation enacted An Ordinance for the Government of the Territory of the United States North-West of the River Ohio, popularly known as the Northwest Ordinance. Adopted on July 13, 1787, the ordinance stated, "There shall be neither slavery nor involuntary servitude in the said territory, otherwise than in the punishment of crimes whereof the party shall have been duly convicted." It was this language that the Republicans in Congress would later copy when drafting the 13th Amendment to abolish slavery nationwide.[26]

Thus, slavery was banned in 1787 from a vast area of the United States, which included the future states of Illinois, Indiana, Michigan, Ohio, Wisconsin, and about a third of Minnesota. In a sign of the times, the Northwest Ordinance was approved by delegations from every state, including every delegate of every slave state.

True, the Northwest Ordinance contained its own fugitive slave clause. But its wording did not reference slavery explicitly. Instead, it referred to "any person escaping into the same, from whom labor or service is lawfully claimed *in any one of the original States*." (Emphasis added.) This reference to "the original States" is significant, for it indicates that going forward, slavery was assumed to exist within only the original states that had not yet abolished it, as opposed to any future states.[27]

This is a remarkable amount of progress toward implementing the political theory of the Declaration in a very short period—a mere 11 years! Yet as we all know, this progress was stopped in its tracks.

Historians generally agree that what stymied this antislavery tide was Eli Whitney's invention of the cotton gin in 1791. By mechanically separating the cotton fiber from the sticky seeds, which formerly had to be done by hand, the plantation farming of cotton using slave labor became enormously profitable. Later, the invention of the steam engine made it feasible to cheaply transport cotton north via the Mississippi and along the coast.

The Constitution was written prior to these technological developments, when slavery was widely viewed as a dying economic institution. After technology made plantation cotton farming highly lucrative, however, for the first time, a proslavery ideology arose in America that increased in its vehemence over time.

But what matters for evaluating the implications of the Declaration adopted by Congress in 1776 for the Constitution of 1787 is not what came soon after the Constitution was drafted. What matters is that the Constitution was written *before* this change occurred. It was written on the cusp of half the states in the union turning away from slavery and the Northwest Ordinance barring slavery in the territories from which six future states would be formed. It was written before an explicitly proslavery ideology arrested what seemed like rapid progress toward a national consensus that was fully consistent with the Declaration's stated principles. In short, when the Constitution was written in 1787, the United States was still on the leading edge of the movement to end the worldwide practice of chattel slavery.

To be sure, some slaveholders, especially in the Deep South, adamantly insisted on preserving slavery. And even those in the South who conceded slavery's injustice had deeply self-interested motives to kick the can of its demise down the road. Much of their wealth was bound up in their slaves. Some of them feared violent retaliation by those persons they had enslaved. But the point remains that at the moment the Constitution was drafted, these resisters were thought to be on the wrong side of history. And they were on the wrong side of history in the long run thanks, in part, to how the Constitution was worded.

Refusing to Endorse Property in Man

The text of the original Constitution reflects this remarkable progress. Nowhere in the document is slavery mentioned by name. This reflects the intellectual consensus that slavery was unjust and would inevitably be no more. Nor, contrary to Taney's claim, does the document "expressly" endorse the morality of slavery or the concept of property in man.[28]

In *No Property in Man*, Wilentz details the lengths to which states from the Deep South went to include an expressed endorsement of slavery in the Constitution. At every turn, a coalition of antislavery Northern delegates and members of the Virginia delegation denied their efforts.

For example, the initial draft of what became the fugitive slave clause of Article IV referred to enslaved people by the same language employed by the Northwest Ordinance: persons "from whom labor or service is *lawfully* claimed" in one of the original states.[29] (Emphasis added.) As Wilentz notes, with this language, "the slave states' property laws would be respected without compelling the free territories to acknowledge the legitimacy of property in man."[30] The day after an extensive debate on the propriety of this clause, Pierce Butler of South Carolina replaced the phrase "lawfully claimed" with the phrase "shall be delivered up to the person *justly* claiming their service or labor."[31] (Emphasis added.) Because the term "justly" would imply not merely the legality but also the justice or morality of the claim to service or labor, the antislavery coalition resisted it.

The delegate who spoke out most vociferously against slavery at the convention was Pennsylvania's Gouverneur Morris, who delivered an impassioned speech on what he called the "nefarious institution" of slavery. Morris insisted that it was "the curse of heaven on the States where it prevailed." Given that Morris was tasked with writing the actual text of the Constitution as a member of the Committee on Style, it would be surprising if the text of the Constitution expressly endorsed the concept of property in man as Taney claimed.[32]

In Morris's hands, the term "justly" was deleted from the fugitive slave clause. But the Committee on Style's draft language still began "No person *legally* held to service or labour in one state." (Emphasis added.) This, too, proved to be unacceptable to the body of the convention when it considered the Constitution's final wording. The language was revised to instead read "No person held to Service or Labour in one State, *under the Laws thereof.*" (Emphasis added.) In his notes, Madison explained that this change was made "in compliance with the wish of some who thought the term *legal* equivocal, and favoring the idea that slavery was legal in a moral view."[33]

In the 19th century, some abolitionists would mobilize the phrase "under the laws thereof" to argue that the Constitution adopted the view of "freedom national" and "slavery local." This distinction was first enunciated by antislavery constitutionalist and Free-Soil Senator Salmon Chase of Ohio in an 1850 Senate speech, which was later published as a pamphlet, titled "Union and Freedom, Without Compromise." When it came to the exercise of its national powers, Chase contended, the federal government was fully empowered to end slavery in its domain. The only protection afforded to slavery by the Constitution was that "any one of the original States"—as the Northwest Ordinance put it—could continue to maintain it solely as a matter of their positive law.[34]

Chase had been sent to the Senate in 1850 after an election had given the Free-Soil Party the swing vote between the Whigs and the Democrats in the Ohio legislature. The Free-Soilers made a deal to give the Democrats control of the legislature in exchange for abolishing Ohio's discriminatory black code and naming Chase a senator. (Some Ohio Whigs would never forgive Chase for making this deal; they would later undercut his candidacy for the 1860 Republican Party presidential nomination, which went to Abraham Lincoln.)

Two years later, a similar deal struck between the Free-Soilers and Massachusetts Democrats sent Charles Sumner to join Chase in the Senate. In 1852, Sumner presented this "Freedom National; Slavery Local" position at length on the floor of the Senate. Sumner's speech received far more attention than had Chase's. After meticulously parsing the debates in Philadelphia, Sumner concluded,

This record demonstrates that the word "person" was employed in order to show that slaves, everywhere under the Constitution, were always to be regarded as persons, and not as property, and thus to exclude from the Constitution all idea that there can be property in man. Remember well, that Mr. Sherman was opposed to the [fugitive slave] clause in its original form, "as acknowledging men to be property;" that Mr. Madison was also opposed to it, because he "thought it wrong to admit in the Constitution the idea that there could be property in man;" and that, after these objections, the clause was so amended as to exclude the idea. But Slavery cannot be national, unless this idea is distinctly and unequivocally admitted into the Constitution.[35]

Instead, slavery was a creature entirely of local law, to be tolerated but in no way endorsed or expanded by the Constitution. This position eventually became the organizing principle of the Republican Party, which Chase helped found. (In 1856 he was elected the governor of Ohio as a Republican.)

The original Constitution also affirmed Congress's power to abolish the slave trade with other nations, though Congress postponed any exercise of this power for 20 years. At the time, antislavery activists considered this a major blow against slavery. In 1808, President Jefferson proposed the abolition of that trade, and Congress swiftly acted to do so.

What power was Congress exercising when it abolished the slave trade? According to Edmund Randolph, the first attorney general, it was Congress's power "to regulate commerce with foreign Nations, and among the several states, and with the Indian tribes."[36] As Randolph explained to the Virginia ratification convention,

To what power in the general government is the exception made respecting the importation of negroes? Not from a general power, but from a particular power expressly enumerated. This is an exception from the power given them of regulating commerce.[37]

Consistent with this interpretation, prior to the abolition of the international slave trade in 1808, Congress exercised its commerce power to enact the Slave Trade Act of 1794, which regulated the international slave trade by barring American flagships from importing or exporting enslaved laborers abroad.[38]

On this reasoning, however, the commerce clause in the original Constitution also gave Congress the power to abolish the *interstate* slave trade. In his 1850 speech to the Senate, Chase made this argument regarding the commerce clause, adding, "Is it less cruel, less deserving of punishment, to tear fathers, mothers, children from their homes and each other, in Maryland and Virginia, and transport them to the markets of Louisiana or Mississippi?"[39]

Then there is the wording of the fugitive slave clause in Article IV. Unlike the Constitution's full faith and credit clause and the republican guarantee clause, the fugitive slave clause lacked a congressional enforcement power. As a young attorney representing fugitive slaves in the 1830s, Chase contended that Congress lacked any enumerated power to enforce what amounts to a treaty obligation of one sovereign state to another. Justice Joseph Story rejected this argument in the 1842 Supreme Court case *Prigg v. Pennsylvania*, which found that Congress could direct the federal judiciary to protect the rights of slave owners seeking to recapture escaped slaves.[40] However, he did so by interpreting the Constitution's necessary and proper clause even more capaciously than did the New Deal and Warren Courts of the 20th century.

Furthermore, Article IV included the enumerated power of Congress to "make all needful Rules and Regulations respecting the Territory or other Property belonging to the United States."[41] Congress also had an enumerated power "to exercise exclusive Legislation in all Cases whatsoever, over" the District of Columbia.[42] These clauses seem obviously to grant Congress the same power to abolish slavery in the territories, on federal government installations, and in the District of Columbia as the seven original states that chose to abolish slavery prior to the Civil War.

The only constitutional objection to this federal power to abolish slavery in these locales was formulated in 1836 in a report by the House Select Committee upon the Subject of Slavery in the District of Columbia, chaired by Representative Henry Pinckney of South Carolina.[43] In its report, the committee claimed that Congress's right to legislate within the district, though exclusive, was "evidently qualified" by the due process clause of the Fifth Amendment.[44]

According to this theory, the due process clause's protection of "life, liberty, and *property*" (emphasis added) limited federal power over the district by preventing it from denying slaveholders of their rightful property in their slaves. This was exactly the argument that Taney would employ some 20 years later in *Dred Scott* in extending the argument to Congress's power over the territories. But, as I have shown, Taney was making it up in *Dred Scott* when he contended that "the right of property in a slave is distinctly and expressly affirmed in the Constitution."[45]

McLean also denied Taney's claim in his dissent, explaining that "we know as a historical fact, that James Madison, that great and good man, a leading member in the Federal Convention, was solicitous to guard the language of that instrument so as not to convey the idea that there could be property in man." McLean might have added that Madison was far from alone in this endeavor. Wilentz shows that, with respect to a majority of the delegates to the Constitutional Convention, McLean was right and Taney was wrong. These delegates went to great lengths to prevent the text of the Constitution from expressly contradicting the Declaration's principles.[46] That effort would later prove useful to antislavery constitutionalists who would assert federal power to limit the spread of slavery as well as to abolish it where the federal government had full authority.

The Republican Party platform of 1860 announced the antislavery policies that Chase had long contended were entirely constitutional. In reading these planks, notice the emphasis on the original meaning of the Constitution's text—that is, "the explicit provisions of that instrument itself, [and its] contemporaneous exposition":

2. That the maintenance of the principles promulgated in the Declaration of Independence and embodied in the Federal Constitution, "That all men are created equal; that they are endowed by their Creator with certain inalienable rights; that among these are life, liberty and the pursuit of happiness; that to secure these rights, governments are instituted among men, deriving their just powers from the consent of the governed," is essential to the preservation of our Republican institutions; and that the Federal Constitution, the Rights of the States, and the Union of the States must and shall be preserved. . . .

7. That the new dogma that the Constitution, of its own force, carries slavery into any or all of the territories of the United States, is a dangerous political heresy, at variance with the explicit provisions of that instrument itself, with contemporaneous exposition, and with legislative and judicial precedent; is revolutionary in its tendency, and subversive of the peace and harmony of the country.

8. That the normal condition of all the territory of the United States is that of freedom: That, as our Republican fathers, when they had abolished slavery in all our national territory, ordained that "no persons should be deprived of life, liberty or property without due process of law," it becomes our duty, by legislation, whenever such legislation is necessary, to maintain this provision of the Constitution against all attempts to violate it; and *we deny the authority of Congress, of a territorial legislature, or of any individuals, to give legal existence to slavery in any territory of the United States.*[47] (Emphasis added.)

Republicans did not believe that the Constitution gave the federal government the power to abolish slavery in any of the six original states in which it still existed; to accomplish this they would come to support an amendment to abolish slavery by 1865. Yet in 1860, their pledge to use federal power to resist the expansion of slavery into the territories, bar slavery on federal installations, and abolish slavery in the District of Columbia (which they achieved in 1862) was perceived by the Southern states to be so grave a threat to their system of human bondage that they seceded from the Union before the new administration could take office. That is how much power the Southerners believed the Constitution gave an antislavery national government to restrict slavery. So they got out while the getting was good.

If the original Constitution was as proslavery as the abolitionist William Lloyd Garrison and Taney had claimed, and as is widely preached today, these fears would have been entirely unwarranted. There would have been no need for the Southern states to secede. But the Southerners were right to be afraid. Immediately after taking office, the Republicans, now unopposed due to the absence of Southern representatives, moved swiftly to enact their policies using the powers granted to Congress by the original Constitution.[48]

As we know, the secession of the Southern slave states led directly to a terrible war that ended slavery in the United States. All this was made possible by the language of the Constitution, which was deliberately shaped by the founding principles of the Declaration of Independence.

Original Meaning Versus Implementation

In the spring of 1851, Frederick Douglass publicly changed his stance on the Constitution, repudiating Garrison's reading that the Constitution was "a covenant with death" and "an agreement with hell" and joining the ranks of the antislavery constitutionalists. In 1860, Douglass was invited to debate the question whether the Constitution was proslavery or antislavery. In his remarks, Douglass took care to distinguish between the *Constitution* of the United States and the *government* of the United States.[49]

In thinking about the original Constitution today, we would be wise to heed Douglass's framing of the issue. The question, he said,

> is not whether slavery existed in the United States at the time
> of the adoption of the Constitution; it is not whether slave-
> holders took part in the framing of the Constitution; it is not
> whether those slaveholders, in their hearts, intended to secure
> certain advantages in that instrument for slavery; it is not
> whether the American Government has been wielded during
> seventy-two years in favour of the propagation and perma-
> nence of slavery; it is not whether a pro-slavery interpretation
> has been put upon the Constitution by the American Courts—
> all these points may be true or they may be false, they may be
> accepted or they may be rejected, without in any wise affecting
> the real question in debate.[50]

According to Douglass, the real question is, "Does the United States Constitution guarantee to any class or description of people in that country the right to enslave, or hold as property, any other class or description of people in that country?"[51] In his answer, Douglass adopted a version of the "original meaning" method of interpretation developed by abolitionist Lysander Spooner in response to activist Wendell Phillips's 1844 pamphlet *The Constitution: A Pro-Slavery Compact; or, Extracts from the Madison Papers, Etc.* As its subtitle reflects, in this tract, Phillips relied on evidence of the original *intentions* of the framers in Philadelphia.[52]

Douglass specifically rejected the original intent approach of those he called "the Garrisonians":

> It should also be borne in mind that the *intentions* of those who
> framed the Constitution, be they good or bad, for slavery or
> against slavery, are respected so far, and so far only, as we find
> those intentions plainly stated in the Constitution. It would
> be the wildest of absurdities, and lead to endless confusion

and mischiefs, if, instead of looking to the written paper itself, for its meaning, it were attempted to make us search it out, in the secret motives, and dishonest intentions, of some of the men who took part in writing it. *It was what they said that was adopted by the people, not what they were ashamed or afraid to say, and really omitted to say.*[53] (Emphasis added.)

Douglass was able to rely on the Declaration's principles when interpreting the text of the Constitution because a majority of the delegates who framed the Constitution went to great lengths to avoid wording that was inconsistent with those abstract principles. But what about the well-known "compromises" with the institution of slavery that did make it into the Constitution? Lest I be accused of gilding the lily, it is important to acknowledge where the founders did go wrong.

Slavery and the Founding

In this chapter, I have only scratched the surface of how the original Constitution contributed to the ultimate demise of slavery. For example, I did not discuss the important role federalism played. Before concluding, however, let me offer three important caveats.

To begin, while the Constitution's original meaning was not proslavery, neither was it *antislavery*. By this I mean the original meaning of the Constitution did not make slavery unconstitutional, as abolitionists such as William Goodell, Gerrit Smith, Spooner, and Joel Tiffany argued. Rather, as Chase contended, the Constitution gave an antislavery national government enough power to put slavery on the road to its extinction.

Second, we cannot deny that the Constitution left slavery as it found it in the original states where it still existed in 1789. Contrary to Spooner, slavery was not unconstitutional under the original Constitution. But to again paraphrase Chase, the original Constitution also gave the federal government ample power to confine slavery within the borders of these states, prevent its further expansion, and indirectly undermine its continued existence.

Slavery grew more powerful in the antebellum period not because of its endorsement by the Constitution but because of the political forces that supported its existence and expansion and how the structure of the original Constitution allowed these forces to dominate the national government. This political domination was abetted by allowing Southern states to count each of their slaves as three-fifths of a person for purposes of representation in Congress, which also enhanced their power in the Electoral College. And it was the president, with the advice and consent of the Senate, who chose the justices of the Supreme Court. Thus, all three branches came under the sway of what antislavery activists called the "Slave Power." This was indeed one of several structural flaws in the original Constitution.

Although the South received less federal representation than it could have achieved if slaves had been counted as full persons, the three-fifths compromise with the slave states still proved disastrous when the economics of slavery changed markedly after the invention of the cotton gin. It enabled the Slave Power to thwart any use of federal power to undermine slavery. But the three-fifths clause cannot take all the blame. It was not responsible for the Northern Democrats, and not a few Northern Whigs, who marched in political lockstep with Southern slaveholders, in some cases due to their profiting by trading the products of slave labor. These people, not the original Constitution, are to blame for failing to utilize the powers that the Constitution gave the national government to all but abolish slavery.

A final and important caveat: Opposing slavery was not the same as rejecting racism or white supremacy. For example, slavery could be opposed because it was thought to compete unfairly with free white labor. Many who opposed slavery also favored the "colonization" of freed slaves in western Africa because they believed racial integration was undesirable, impractical, or both. If the 13th Amendment was needed to abolish slavery, the 14th and 15th Amendments were needed to combat the system of coercive white supremacy that remained embedded after slavery's demise. But neither should we forget that many opponents of slavery, like Chase, were motivated by liberal convictions regarding racial equality.

Ultimately, the founding's achievements—both the Declaration and the Constitution—proved immensely valuable in combating the moral scourge of slavery. At the 250th anniversary of the Declaration of Independence, Americans should be far more aware of both antislavery constitutionalism and how the antislavery Republican Party amended the Constitution to end slavery and then amended it again to combat white supremacy. But so too should we be far more aware of how much the founding generation opposed slavery in principle and planted the seeds of its undoing in the text of the original Constitution they drafted and ratified.

The abolition of slavery was an accomplishment of which Americans should be proud. And it was greatly aided and abetted by the Declaration of Independence. Critics of the Declaration should think twice before they adopt the views of Roger Taney as their own.

Notes

1. See Randy E. Barnett, "The Declaration of Independence and the American Theory of Government: 'First Come Rights, and Then Comes Government,'" *Harvard Journal of Law & Public Policy* 42, no. 1 (2019): 23–28, https://journals.law.harvard.edu/jlpp/wp-content/uploads/sites/90/2019/02/Barnett-FINAL.pdf.

2. See, for example, Robert G. Parkinson, "You Can't Tell the Story of 1776 Without Talking About Race and Slavery," *Time*, July 4, 2021, https://time.com/6077468/united-states-1776-racism-slavery/. ("Slavery and arguments about race were not only at the heart of the American founding; it was what united the states in the first place.")

3. Dred Scott v. Sandford, 60 US 393, 407 (1857).

4. *Dred Scott*, 60 US at 407.

5. For an overview of the theory of originalism and its development since the 1980s, see Randy E. Barnett and Evan Bernick, "The Letter and the Spirit: A Unified Theory of Originalism," *The Georgetown Law Journal* 107, no. 1 (2018): 1–55, https://www.

law.georgetown.edu/georgetown-law-journal/wp-content/uploads/sites/26/2018/12/
The-Letter-and-the-Spirit-1.pdf.

6. *Dred Scott*, 60 US at 410.

7. *Dred Scott*, 60 US at 410.

8. Ironically, when today's critics echo Taney's claim, they are adopting original intent originalism, a version of originalism that was widely criticized by non-originalists and has been abandoned by most originalists. See Barnett and Bernick, "The Letter and the Spirit," 9–10, 45–46.

9. *Dred Scott*, 60 US at 421.

10. *Dred Scott*, 60 US at 537 (McLean, J., dissenting).

11. *Dred Scott*, 60 US at 574 (Curtis, J., dissenting).

12. *Dred Scott*, 60 US at 574.

13. *Dred Scott*, 60 US at 574.

14. *Dred Scott*, 60 US at 574–75.

15. *Dred Scott*, 60 US at 575. The definition of American citizenship was left largely to individual states until the Civil Rights Act of 1866 and the passage of the 14th Amendment. See Eric Foner, *The Second Founding: How the Civil War and Reconstruction Remade the Constitution* (W. W. Norton, 2019), 3, 63, 70.

16. Worthington Chauncey Ford, ed., *Journals of the Continental Congress, 1774–1789*, vol. 5, *1776: June 5–October 8* (Government Printing Office, 1906), 429, quoted in Pauline Maier, *American Scripture: Making the Declaration of Independence* (Alfred A. Knopf, 1997), 126.

17. John Hancock to Certain States, July 6, 1776, quoted in Maier, *American Scripture*.

18. Maier, *American Scripture*, 43, 97–99.

19. Maier, *American Scripture*, 103.

20. Maier, *American Scripture*, 125–26.

21. Virginia Declaration of Rights, *The Pennsylvania Gazette*, June 12, 1776, quoted in Maier, *American Scripture*, 126–27.

22. Virginia Declaration of Rights, in Maier, *American Scripture*, 127.

23. Sean Wilentz, *No Property in Man: Slavery and Antislavery at the Nation's Founding* (Harvard University Press, 2018), 25.

24. Vt. Const. of 1777, ch. I, art. 1.

25. Wilentz, *No Property in Man*, 30.

26. Northwest Ordinance of 1787, art. VI.

27. Northwest Ordinance of 1787, art. VI. True, in 1790, Congress enacted the Southwest Ordinance to govern the territories ceded to the United States by North Carolina, from which the states of Kentucky and Tennessee were formed in 1792 and 1796, respectively. In that law, Congress obliquely adopted the provision of the North Carolina cession act that debarred Congress from abolishing slavery in states formed from this territory. But this was the preservation of the status quo with respect to that land, not an extension of slavery into new areas. That there were many in the South who ardently wished to preserve their unjust dominion (while often conceding its

injustice) is undeniable. The issue here is whether the Declaration's original meaning was inherently antislavery, a reading the Northwest Ordinance supports.

28. *Dred Scott*, 60 US at 425 ("The only two provisions which point to them and include them, treat them as property"), 451 ("The right of property in a slave is distinctly and *expressly* affirmed in the Constitution"). (Emphasis added.)

29. Northwest Ordinance of 1787, art. VI. See also Act of Aug. 7, 1789, ch. 8, 1 Stat. 50, 51–53.

30. Wilentz, *No Property in Man*, 105.

31. *Debates in the Federal Convention of 1787 by James Madison, a Member*, ed. Gordon Lloyd (Ashbrook Center, 2014), 454.

32. Wilentz, *No Property in Man*, 77.

33. Wilentz, *No Property in Man*, 110–12; and *Debates in the Federal Convention of 1787 by James Madison, a Member*, 542. The latter meaning of "legal" reflected the dominance of natural law thinking at the time. The term "law" was equivocal as it was commonly used then, as today, to refer to a statute or legislative "act," as distinct from a morally binding law.

34. Salmon Chase, "Union and Freedom, Without Compromise," speech, US Senate, Washington, DC, March 26, 1850.

35. Charles Sumner, *Freedom National; Slavery Sectional* (Washington, DC, 1852), 20.

36. US Const. art. I, § 8, cl. 3.

37. Jonathan Elliot, ed., *The Debates in the Several State Conventions on the Adoption of the Federal Constitution* [...], 2nd ed. (Washington, DC, 1863), 3:464. See Randy E. Barnett, "The Original Meaning of the Commerce Clause," *The University of Chicago Law Review* 68, no. 1 (2001): 143, https://chicagounbound.uchicago.edu/cgi/viewcontent.cgi?article=5074&context=uclrev.

38. 1 Stat. 347.

39. Chase, "Union and Freedom, Without Compromise." Few asserted this interpretation of the text in the 1800s, however, because of the implications of such a reading for preserving the union, which is not relevant to its original meaning.

40. See Prigg v. Pennsylvania, 41 US 539 (1842).

41. US Const. art. IV, § 3, cl. 2.

42. US Const. art. I, § 8, cl. 17.

43. See Randy E. Barnett, *Whence Comes Section One? The Abolitionist Origins of the Fourteenth Amendment, Journal of Legal Analysis* 3, no. 1 (2011): 165, 179–82, https://scholarship.law.georgetown.edu/cgi/viewcontent.cgi?article=1475&context=facpub.

44. H. L. Pinckney, *Report of the Select Committee upon the Subject of Slavery in the District of Columbia* [...] (Washington, DC, 1836), 10.

45. *Dred Scott*, 60 US at 451.

46. *Dred Scott*, 60 US at 537 (McLean, J., dissenting); and Wilentz, *No Property in Man*, 2. As the Constitution's wordsmith, Morris may deserve more credit for this fastidiousness than Madison.

47. University of California, Santa Barbara, American Presidency Project, "Republican Party Platform of 1860," https://www.presidency.ucsb.edu/node/273296.

48. See James Oakes, *Freedom National: The Destruction of Slavery in the United States, 1861–1865* (W. W. Norton, 2014).

49. Wilentz, *No Property in Man*, 12, 274n21.

50. Frederick Douglass, "The American Constitution and the Slave: An Address Delivered in Glasgow, Scotland, on 26 March 1860," in *The Frederick Douglass Papers, Speeches, Debates, and Interviews*, ed. John W. Blassingame, vol. 3, *1855–63* (Yale University Press, 1985), 365.

51. Douglass, "The American Constitution and the Slave," 365.

52. See Lysander Spooner, *The Unconstitutionality of Slavery* (Boston, 1845). Spooner was responding to Wendell Phillips, ed., *The Constitution: a Pro-Slavery Compact: Or, Extracts from the Madison Papers, Etc.* (Boston, 1844). After a lengthy published reply by Phillips, Spooner added a *Part Second* to his book in which he expanded on his interpretative methodology. See Lysander Spooner, *The Unconstitutionality of Slavery*, rev. ed. (Boston, 1860), in *The Collected Works of Lysander Spooner*, ed. Charles Shively, vol. 4, *Anti-Slavery Writings* (M & S Press, 1971), 218. ("It is the *original meaning* of the constitution itself that we are now seeking for.") (Emphasis added.)

53. Douglass, "The American Constitution and the Slave," 366.

2

Freedom and Federalism

KURT T. LASH

The Declaration of Independence contains two key principles of American liberty: individual freedom and structural federalism. First, every person has an equal right to life, liberty, and the pursuit of happiness. Second, the American people have the right to enjoy these liberties in a union composed of free and independent states. Although we often remember and rightly celebrate the first principle, we also should appreciate how the second has advanced the first. The abolition of chattel slavery, for example, resulted from successful mobilization in the "free and independent states"—a mobilization that would have been thwarted and crushed absent the structural protection of constitutional federalism.

American independence gave birth to federalism, and federalism facilitated a new birth of freedom that culminated in the adoption of the 13th and 14th Amendments. Shallow historical narratives often associate states' rights with the proslavery South. But Madisonian federalism provided a constitutional shelter under which the Declaration's principle of free and equal men could take political root in the antebellum North. The grassroots antislavery movement that emerged in the Northern states successfully resisted Southern efforts to nationalize slavery and ultimately gave birth to the Republican Party—the first major political party in world history devoted to abolishing slavery. When Republicans prevailed in the 1860 presidential election, proslavery Southern Democrats abandoned James Madison's Constitution and demanded the right to secede from the Union. And war came.

Once the Union army had defeated the Confederacy on the battlefield, Republicans adopted two key amendments that advanced freedom while preserving constitutional federalism. The 13th Amendment secured the Declaration's self-evident truth that no man was born to be the slave of another. The 14th Amendment secured the Declaration's natural rights of life and liberty. Both amendments presumed and relied on the Constitution's federalist structure.

Amendments were necessary *because* moderate Republicans continued to believe in Madisonian federalism and a national government of limited power. Instead of following the preference of radical Republicans like Thaddeus Stevens and Charles Sumner by forcing legislation on defeated "territories," moderate Republicans successfully demanded that constitutional change occur through the federalist mechanism of Article V—ratification by the states. Even the 15th Amendment, which prohibited the denial of voting rights based on color, left the basic mechanics of voting to state control. The content of these amendments maintained the basic divides between national and state law in all matters except those established in the Declaration or enumerated in the Bill of Rights.

Slavery and the Founding

Before the Declaration of Independence, chattel slavery existed throughout North America. Slavery was endemic among the Indigenous peoples of the interior,[1] routinely practiced by the Spanish in the Southwest,[2] and official British policy in the Atlantic colonies.[3]

By the Revolution, however, one finds evidence of a nascent abolitionist movement in the Atlantic colonies. For example, one year before the signing of the Declaration of Independence, Pennsylvanian colonists established the Society for the Relief of Free Negroes Unlawfully Held in Bondage—the first antislavery association in the history of the world.[4] Following their declared separation from Britain, several Northern states began dismantling local laws permitting slavery. In 1777, the people of Vermont adopted a constitution declaring "all men born equally free and independent."[5] Connecticut, Pennsylvania, and Rhode Island also passed acts calling for the gradual abolition of slavery.[6] By 1787, five Northern states (and states-to-be) had officially moved against slavery.[7]

While Northern states increasingly outlawed slavery, states in the Deep South maintained the institution. This regional divide deepened when Congress passed the 1787 Northwest Ordinance, which declared that "there shall be neither slavery nor involuntary servitude in the said territory, otherwise than in the punishment of crimes whereof the party shall have been duly convicted."[8] Originally drafted by Thomas Jefferson,[9] this clause effectively guaranteed that any state carved out of the free Northwest Territory would enter the Union as a free state.[10]

The same summer that Congress passed the Northwest Ordinance, the Philadelphia Convention drafted a new constitution. The original "Articles of Confederation and perpetual Union between the States" failed to sufficiently "provide for the common defense . . . and secure the blessings of liberty."[11] The new constitution advanced these goals by way of a more robust central government but did so in a manner that preserved the basic structure of American federalism—that is, "a Union between the States." As "Publius" wrote in *Federalist* 45, the powers of the national government would be "few and defined," while those left to the states would be "numerous and indefinite."[12]

The few and defined powers of the national government did not include national control of slavery. Although the Constitution made provision for the return of fugitive slaves,[13] the document said nothing about slavery itself—indeed, not even the *word* "slave" appeared in the text. The omission was intentional. As Madison explained during the drafting debates, he "thought it wrong to admit in the Constitution the idea that there could be property in men."[14] Whether to allow or forbid slavery remained a matter presumably reserved to the states, along with a host of additional unenumerated matters, including the regulation of speech and religion.

Critics of the proposed Constitution were unwilling to leave the matter to an unstated presumption and demanded the addition of an express bill of rights like those that accompanied most state constitutions. The proponents of the Constitution conceded the issue, and they promised to add such a bill to the ratified document. In 1791, the states ratified the first 10 amendments to the Constitution—otherwise known as our Bill of Rights. The Bill of Rights includes provisions securing the natural rights of speech and religion through the First Amendment and guaranteeing the due protection of life and liberty through the Fifth Amendment.

The Bill of Rights closes with two amendments that expressly declare the federalist nature of the Constitution. The Ninth Amendment prevents the addition of the Bill of Rights from implying unlimited national power.[15] The 10th Amendment then declares that all powers not delegated to the federal government remain where they were before the Constitution's adoption: with the people of the still free and independent states.[16]

When read through the clarifying lens of the Bill of Rights, the new federal Constitution established a remarkable compound government, one neither wholly federal nor wholly national.[17] A federalist experiment untested in world history, its framers hoped to create a national government powerful enough to defend the nation in a dangerous world and rationalize trade between the states while capturing the democratic benefits of local self-government.

The liberty-enhancing idea of separating power between competing branches at the national level is well-known—this is the Madisonian theory of checks and balances.[18] Less appreciated is the related Madisonian theory that liberty is also enhanced by separating the powers of national and state governments. Maintaining these separate spheres of authority ensured both an ongoing competition between federal and state governments for the people's affection and a vigilant and jealous eye on their governmental rival.[19] As Madison wrote in *Federalist* 44, should the national government attempt to escape its constitutional limits, the states stood ready to "sound the alarm to the people"[20] and mobilize local resistance against tyranny.

In fact, one of the country's first serious constitutional disputes involved an attempted overreach by the national government that prompted just such an alarm. In 1798, Congress passed the Alien and Sedition Acts.[21] Ostensibly meant to quell foreign interference in national politics, the Sedition Act was a bald-faced effort by John Adams's Federalist administration to suppress political speech critical of the national government. As the first federal misinformation law, the act criminalized any speech falsely impugning the actions or character of the national government, with punishment including imprisonment or thousands of dollars in fines.[22] Thankfully, the Constitution preserved the existence of independent states where people remained free to protest unconstitutional legislation. Madison and Jefferson drafted resolutions declaring the acts unconstitutional and had them delivered on the floor of the Virginia and Kentucky legislative assemblies.[23]

According to Madison's "Report on the Virginia Resolutions," published in 1800, the Sedition Act unconstitutionally regulated speech—a matter expressly denied to the federal government and reserved to the states in the First and 10th Amendments of the Bill of Rights.[24] In response to claims that only the national Supreme Court had the authority to determine the constitutionality of congressional acts, Madison noted that the Supreme Court was part of the national government and therefore was as capable of overreaching as any other federal branch.[25] Indeed, the Court would overreach catastrophically only a few decades later in *Dred Scott v. Sandford*.[26]

Madison's arguments in the Virginia Resolutions and the attendant report won the day, if not in federal court, then in the court of public opinion.[27] In the national elections of 1800, the Federalist Party suffered a landslide defeat and was replaced by Madison and Jefferson's new political party: the Democratic-Republicans.[28] As a result, the country entered its first full century broadly committed to the constitutional principles of Madisonian federalism.[29] The liberty to freely and openly dissent from the national government and national policies and do so from the safety of the independent states was now written into the nation's cultural DNA. That liberty would be critical to the successful rise of Northern state-level abolitionism.

Federalism and Abolitionism

One possible outcome of the federalist treatment of slavery under the Constitution was a political balance between pro-freedom and proslavery states. Instead, proslavery states used their disproportionate representation in the federal government to nationalize slavery and suppress pro-freedom state resistance. According to Article IV of the federal Constitution,

> no person held to service or labour in one State, under the laws thereof, escaping into another, shall, in consequence of any law or regulation therein, be discharged from such service or labour, but shall be delivered up on claim of the party to whom such service or labour may be due.[30]

Despite lacking any express grant of federal power for this purpose, in 1793 Congress passed the first Fugitive Slave Act.[31] The act permitted slave owners to pursue their escaped "property" within the boundaries of free states and judicially authorized rendition with nothing more than a signed affidavit.[32]

To protect their free black residents from being wrongly seized and carried into slavery, several Northern states passed "personal freedom laws," which provided due process protections for the accused. For example, Pennsylvania criminalized the removal of any black resident to carry them into slavery and provided a judicial process for persons accused of being a runaway slave.[33] If such laws also protected actual refugees, all the better: Abolitionists insisted that the federal Fugitive Slave Act exceeded Congress's constitutional authority.[34]

In *Prigg v. Pennsylvania*, a nationalist-minded Supreme Court upheld the federal Fugitive Slave Act and invalidated the states' attempt to criminalize its enforcement.[35] Although a blow to state efforts to resist federal law, the *Prigg* decision contained a federalist silver lining. According to Justice Joseph Story, states remained free to prohibit state officials from assisting in the enforcement of the Fugitive Slave Act.[36] Predictably, free states quickly passed laws prohibiting local officials from assisting in slave renditions. More controversially, state officials often declined to punish residents who (sometimes violently) thwarted the efforts of would-be slave catchers.[37]

Absent the protections of structural federalism, the antebellum abolitionist movement likely would have suffocated under a blanket of proslavery nationalism. Between the founding and the Civil War, proslavery interests dominated the national government. The Constitution's three-fifths clause gave a representational bonus to slaveholding states, increasing their political power in Congress and the Electoral College. The result was an almost unbroken line of slave-owning antebellum presidents and a series of federal actions supporting slavery and suppressing abolitionism.[38]

In addition to the Fugitive Slave Acts of 1793 and 1850, Congress passed gag rules in the 1830s and 1840s prohibiting the receipt of abolitionist petitions.[39] Federal officials also purged the national mail of abolitionist literature.[40] Although the Missouri Compromise of 1820 attempted to balance the future admission of slave and free states, the Kansas-Nebraska Act of 1854 violated the compromise and allowed either state to establish slavery.[41] Finally, in *Dred Scott v. Sandford*, the Supreme Court ruled that the Missouri Compromise was an unconstitutional attempt to limit slavery, denied the right of black Americans to invoke the jurisdiction of national courts, and declared the right of slave owners to carry their property into any national territory.[42]

In short, without federalism providing a safe haven for pro-freedom interests in the Northern states, a proslavery national government could have crushed local abolitionist dissent. Instead, Northern abolitionism expanded and diversified.

Initially, abolitionists viewed the Constitution with deep skepticism and moral condemnation. Antebellum abolitionists like William Lloyd Garrison and Wendell Phillips denounced the Constitution as a "pro-slavery compact," and they called for Northern state separation from an "agreement with hell."[43] Over time, however, a more moderate wing of the movement emerged that viewed the Constitution in a more positive light. Abolitionists like Lysander Spooner, Joel Tiffany, and Frederick Douglass insisted that the Constitution could and *should* be interpreted as a pro-freedom document.

These "constitutional abolitionists"[44] insisted that the federal document be read through the lens of the Declaration of Independence, the Northwest Ordinance, and the Bill of Rights—documents they insisted represented the founding generation's intent. The Declaration announced every person's right to life, liberty, and the pursuit of happiness. The Northwest Ordinance illustrated the founders' opposition to the spread of slavery. The Fifth Amendment in the Bill of Rights committed the federal government to basic principles of due process. These documents established the pro-freedom context in which the Constitution was drafted and originally understood. According to this view, the omission of the word "slavery" from the Constitution was neither an accident nor a dodge. It represented an understanding that all texts should be read according to the principles of freedom announced in the Declaration.

The link between the Declaration and the Constitution became standard abolitionist political rhetoric. For example, the 1843 Liberty Party Platform declared

> That the fundamental truths of the Declaration of Independence, that all men are endowed by their Creator with certain inalienable rights, among which are life, liberty and the pursuit of happiness, was made the fundamental law of our national government, by that amendment to the Constitution which declares that no person shall be deprived of life, liberty or property without due process of law. . . . [Slavery is] strictly local, and that its existence and continuance rests on no other support than state legislation.[45]

The Free Soil Party platform similarly invoked the Declaration of Independence and the Fifth Amendment's due process clause, along with the federalist principle that slavery's "existence depends upon the state law alone."[46]

By characterizing slavery as "strictly local"—a matter of federalism—antislavery politicians could claim to respect the states' authority to choose slavery or freedom while opposing the extension of slavery into the territories. As the 1860 Republican Party Platform declared:

> That the maintenance of the principles promulgated in the Declaration of Independence and embodied in the Federal Constitution, "That all men are created equal; that they are endowed by their Creator with certain inalienable rights; that among these are life, liberty and the pursuit of happiness;" . . . and that the Federal Constitution, the Rights of the States, and the Union of the States must and shall be preserved. . . .
>
> That the normal condition of all the territory of the United States is that of freedom: That, as our Republican fathers, when they had abolished slavery in all our national territory, ordained that "no person should be deprived of life, liberty or property without due process of law."[47]

When Abraham Lincoln's election to the presidency triggered threats of secession by Southern slave states, Congress tried to coax continued loyalty to the Union by passing an amendment guaranteeing every state's right to decide the slavery issue for itself.[48] Lincoln himself noted in his inaugural address that he had "no objection" to the proposed amendment since it represented what he already believed to be "implied constitutional law."[49] Although it might seem startling to think Lincoln would acquiesce to an amendment protecting slavery in Southern states, the amendment's language equally protected the right of Northern states to *resist* slavery. It also left unaddressed the federal power to abolish slavery in the territories. No wonder the incoming Republican president had "no objection"! The amendment represented the Republican strategy for geographically limiting and strangling the institution of slavery.

The Southern slave states, of course, recognized that the amendment simply preserved what they believed to be an untenable status quo. One by one, Southern legislatures voted to secede from the Union.[50] Having failed to establish protections for slave owners throughout the United States (a violation of Madisonian federalism), the so-called Confederate States of America now insisted on a unilateral right to exit the Union (another violation of Madisonian federalism).

Secessionism, a radical states' rights theory associated with John C. Calhoun,[51] denied the two key principles of the Declaration. First, since some men could be enslaved, not all men were created equal. Second, by seeking to curb the North's ability to resist slavery's encroachment, secessionists denied the American people the right to live in a union composed of free and independent states.[52]

Had the rebellious state legislatures been satisfied to recall their representatives from Congress, matters might have ultimately found a peaceful political resolution. But when secessionists moved on federal armories and South Carolina fired on Fort Sumter, civil war became inevitable.

A war to end a rebellion, however, is not necessarily a war to end slavery. A quick defeat of the Confederacy, as many in the North expected, would have achieved nothing other than restoring the status quo ante— slavery in the South, freedom in the North, federalism all around. Even as late as 1864, it was still possible that Union voters might replace Lincoln with General George McClellan, who promised to bring a quick end to the war on terms agreeable to the South.[53] Only miraculously timed military victories that summer and fall prevented such an electoral disaster.[54] Lincoln thus began his second term with a popular mandate to *win* the Civil War. He would use that mandate in a manner that permanently grafted the principles of the Declaration into the text of the Constitution.

The Reconstruction Amendments and Jefferson's Declaration

Fearing that a Supreme Court that still had a Democratic majority could eventually threaten the Emancipation Proclamation, neither Lincoln nor congressional Republicans were willing to wait for the end of the Civil War before pursuing the adoption of an abolition amendment. Republicans drafted the 13th Amendment in early 1864 and secured its passage in January 1865—months before Robert E. Lee's surrender at Appomattox.[55] For the amendment's text, Republicans drew from the well of the nation's founding and used Jefferson's language prohibiting slavery in the Northwest Territory. Here are the two texts side by side:

- The Northwest Ordinance: "There shall be neither slavery nor involuntary servitude in the said territory, otherwise than in the punishment of crimes whereof the party shall have been duly convicted."[56]

- The 13th Amendment: "Neither slavery nor involuntary servitude, except as a punishment for crime whereof the party shall have been duly convicted, shall exist within the United States."[57]

By using the language of the Northwest Ordinance, Republicans bolstered their claim that the amendment shared a lineage with Jefferson's Declaration and their pro-freedom interpretation of the Constitution. It was freedom, not slavery, that defined America.

Although the 13th Amendment abolished the institution, slavery's malignant spirit still roamed the land in the form of Southern Black Codes—laws that denied the equal protection of every person's life, liberty, and property. Abolitionists had long understood the Fifth Amendment's protection of life, liberty, and property as having constitutionalized the basic principles of the Declaration of Independence.[58] The Bill of Rights, however, bound the federal government, not the states.

After much deliberation, Republicans proposed the 14th Amendment. This provision would further expand the Constitution's commitment to the Declaration's principles. If *all* men were created equal, then every person born on American soil and within its jurisdiction had an equal right to American citizenship. In language casting the *Dred Scott* ruling into eternal obloquy, the 14th Amendment declares that "*all* persons born or naturalized in the United States and subject to the jurisdiction thereof are citizens of the United States, and of the state wherein they reside." Henceforth, no state could enact any code denying resident black citizens the same rights as resident white citizens.[59]

Next, the 14th Amendment asserts that no person, citizen or not, can be deprived of life, liberty, or property without due process of law. In doing so, the amendment applied the Declaration's natural rights claims to the people in the states. If all men held the inalienable right to life, liberty, and happiness, then neither the national government *nor any state* may wrongly deprive any person of their life, liberty, or property. Furthermore, if all men are created equal, then their life, liberty, and property should be equally protected. Therefore, no state may "deny to any person within its jurisdiction the *equal* protection of the laws." (Emphasis added.) This "equal protection of the laws" clause requires states to provide black residents the same protection against mob violence as white residents.[60]

Lincoln once noted that the Declaration of Independence is America's "apple of gold" and the Constitution is "the picture of silver, subsequently framed around it."[61] The 13th and 14th Amendments make Lincoln's simile all the more true. In particular, the language and principles of the Declaration of Independence are everywhere in the 14th Amendment. All persons, having been created equal, have equal rights of state and national citizenship. All persons, created with equal inalienable rights, must be equally free in exercising those rights.

Federalism and Reconstruction

The defeat of the Confederacy was a defeat for Calhoun's radical states' rights theory. Secessionists claimed that the Constitution was merely a federal compact that any sufficiently aggrieved signatory could unilaterally abrogate. They drew on the theory of nullification outlined in Jefferson's Kentucky Resolutions to justify their separation from the Union. Although they also cited Madison's Virginia Resolutions in support of their views, secessionists ignored—or simply disagreed with—the arguments Madison made as "Publius" in the Federalist Papers that the Constitution was neither wholly national nor wholly federal. Indeed, Calhoun insisted that Publius had been wrong to make such a claim.[62]

To Northern Republicans, the defeat of the Confederacy represented a defeat of constitutional heresy and a victory for Madisonian federalism. Between the founding and the Civil War, the Federalist Papers had emerged as the most broadly respected source on the original understanding of the Constitution.[63] In those essays, Publius assured the states that, in all matters not delegated to the federal government, they remained "free and independent." No state would be forced to join the Union. For example, if North Carolina declined to ratify the proposed Constitution, then it would remain outside the Union as a wholly sovereign and independent state. But once the people of a state voted to ratify the Constitution, from then on, that state and its people became a constituent part of a new Union.

Ratification brought into being a wholly new political invention—one nation composed of two spheres of authority, state and federal. Following ratification, the only constitutional method of settling disputes over slavery or anything else required following Article V's amendment procedures. For Republicans, nothing about the Civil War or the abolition of slavery altered this basic federalist structure. As the Republican Chief Justice Salmon P. Chase explained in the 1869 decision *Texas v. White*, which found that states could not unilaterally secede from the Union, "The Constitution in all its provisions, looks to an indestructible Union, composed of indestructible states."[64] Chase presents the two-edged sword of federalism: Neither could states destroy the Union through secession nor could the Union destroy the states through unabridged nationalism. *Both* sides of federalism remained critically important in the aftermath of the Civil War.

Radical Republicans would have happily jettisoned American federalism and imposed their will on the defeated South. The state-suicide theory of radicals like Sumner and Stevens envisioned a new "southern territory" under the full regulatory control of Congress.[65] If they had prevailed, no additional amendments would have been necessary. Congress could have banned slavery, passed a civil rights code, and enfranchised black Americans in the Southern states, all without having to undertake the arduous effort of convincing three-quarters of both Northern and Southern states to amend the Constitution. However, while legislation could secure black rights in the short term, passing constitutional amendments protected these rights in the long term.[66]

The fact that most of the country rejected radical Republican nationalism, choosing instead to pursue amendments in accordance with Article V's requirements, also illustrates how deeply entwined federalism and freedom had become between the founding and the Civil War. Throughout the debates of the Reconstruction Congress, we find moderate Republicans insisting that the country remained a federalist union of states. Freedom in the South had to be secured before the readmission of Southern congressmen, but that freedom had to be secured by way of *state*-ratified amendments.

John Bingham, the primary author of Section 1 of the 14th Amendment, notably refused to support the 1866 Civil Rights Act because Congress had no enumerated power to enforce equal rights of life, liberty, and property. Bingham agreed with the goals of civil rights legislation, but he insisted that pursuing those goals required a new amendment. Until that happened, constitutional federalism prohibited the very legislation Congress was trying to pass.

In his speech proposing a 14th Amendment, Bingham quoted Madison's *Federalist* 45: "The powers reserved to the several States will extend to all the objects which, in the ordinary course of affairs, concern the lives, liberties, and properties of the people, and the internal order, improvement, and prosperity of the State." This Madisonian principle, Bingham declared, was written into "the very text of the Constitution itself" in the 10th Amendment.[67] What was needed was an amendment legally obligating the states to respect the federal Bill of Rights—something they had a moral obligation to do anyway.[68] Over and over again, Bingham insisted the proposed amendment would leave intact the original federalist arrangement between the states and national government. He sought enforcement of the Bill of Rights at the state level—and nothing more.[69]

Although Congress passed the 14th Amendment, for a time it remained unclear whether enough states would vote for its ratification. Midway through the ratification process, a restless Stevens tried to convince his colleagues to abandon the amendment process and simply pass a statute accomplishing the same result.[70] Once again, it was Bingham who stood up for the principle of limited national power and the independence of the states from federal control:

> Sir, I am not to be thus driven into a violation of the letter and spirit of the Constitution of the country. Under it the rights of the States are as sacred as those of the nation; its express provision is that—
>
> > "The powers not delegated to the United States by the Constitution, nor prohibited by it to the States, are reserved to the States respectively, or to the people." . . .
>
> The equality of the States and the equality of men in the rights of person before the law is what the Constitution enjoins and the people demand.[71]

Bingham's repeated citations of Madison and the 10th Amendment were not at all unusual. One can find similar examples throughout the debates over the three Reconstruction amendments. Republicans of all stripes cited the Federalist Papers as authoritative statements of the nature of the postbellum Constitution. The same members who excoriated Calhoun's radical states' rights theories also cited Publius's federalist theories as the basis for a functioning constitutional system.

In the end, Bingham convinced his colleagues to stay the course and allow the people in the states to decide whether to ratify the amendment. Instead of radical Republican efforts to erase the states, Bingham and his colleagues passed the Reconstruction Acts of 1867, which allowed both black and white voters in the Southern states to vote on new constitutions and new state governments—state governments that would hold new votes on ratifying the 14th Amendment. Calhoun and slavery were dead, but freedom and federalism remained very much alive.

Freedom and Federalism Today

The principles of freedom and federalism articulated by the Declaration of Independence have informed American constitutional liberty for 250 years. The 13th Amendment constitutionalized the Declaration's assertion of human equality by abolishing slavery and empowering Congress to prohibit its "badges and incidents"—power enforced by federal statutes prohibiting racial discrimination in contracts and real estate purchases.[72] The 14th Amendment requires states to equally protect every person's life, liberty, and property and guarantees equal civil rights to every American citizen. The Supreme Court enforced these provisions through cases on education access like *Brown v. Board of Education* and *Students for Fair Admissions v. Harvard*.[73] In the mid-20th century, the Supreme Court also belatedly realized Bingham's vision of a national Bill of Rights by interpreting the due process clause of the 14th Amendment as having incorporated much of the first eight amendments. The Declaration's vision of individual freedom, in other words, is now a foundational aspect of American law.

So too is structural federalism. In the 1990s, the Supreme Court reinvigorated what had been a moribund 10th Amendment. In cases like *New York v. United States* and *United States v. Lopez*, the Supreme Court drew on the 10th Amendment to impose limits on the power Congress could derive from the Constitution's commerce clause.[74] In his majority opinion for *Bond v. United States*,[75] Justice Anthony Kennedy cited several Supreme Court cases to conclude that the 10th Amendment's restrictions exist not for the protection of the states, but for the protection of individual Americans. As Kennedy wrote:

> The federal system rests on what might at first seem a counterintuitive insight, that "freedom is enhanced by the creation of two governments, not one." *Alden* v. *Maine*, 527 U. S. 706, 758 (1999). The Framers concluded that allocation of powers between the National Government and the States enhances freedom, first by protecting the integrity of the governments themselves, and second by protecting the people, from whom all governmental powers are derived. . . .
>
> . . . "State sovereignty is not just an end in itself: 'Rather, federalism secures to citizens the liberties that derive from the diffusion of sovereign power.'" *New York* v. *United States*, 505 U. S. 144, 181 (1992) (quoting *Coleman* v. *Thompson*, 501 U. S. 722, 759 (1991) (Blackmun, J., dissenting)).[76]

Kennedy's opinion echoes Bingham's praise of federalism during the drafting of the 14th Amendment. It also echoes the liberty principle of structural federalism embedded in the Declaration, the Constitution, and the 14th Amendment. The 10th Amendment merely declared what was already the framers' understanding of the Constitution before the adoption of the Bill of Rights. As Publius explained, the Constitution retained the Declaration's free and independent states as constituent parts of its dual federalist structure.[77] Similarly, the 14th Amendment's drafters insisted that the privileges and immunities of American citizenship included those listed in *all 10* amendments of the Bill of Rights.[78]

The 10th Amendment ultimately played a key role in advancing American liberty. Madison would have predicted as much—separation of powers and federalism represent a "double security" for the protection of individual rights.[79] In the 19th century, structural federalism permitted and assisted the rise of Northern abolitionism. However, states' rights became a byword for injustice during the 1950s when racist, segregated states engaged in "massive resistance" against the Supreme Court's order to desegregate public schools.[80] But these modern efforts of interposition and nullification echoed Calhounian radicalism, not Madisonian federalism. Nullification theory, as Madison explained long ago, violates the dual federalist agreement, which the states themselves ratified in 1787.[81] Violation and obstruction of federal law are not the correspondence among the states envisioned by Madison in his Virginia Resolutions but instead involve the same unilateral rejection of the people's Constitution attempted by secessionists.

Madisonian federalism envisions local *political* dissent and the opportunity to build local and regional political coalitions. These political activities by free and independent states deepen political engagement across the country and facilitate the creation of new democratic majorities. Constitutional text represents those issues that the people have debated and collectively chosen to entrench as fundamental law. But not every subject has been constitutionalized. Indeed, not even all the most important subjects have been constitutionalized. The country remains divided over issues involving preborn human life, the significance of biological sex, the care of the environment, the scope of parental rights, and many other areas either absent from or unclearly covered by the Constitution.

The national diktats handed down through judicial rulings in cases like *Dred Scott v. Sandford* and *Roe v. Wade* attempt to artificially end public debate. It is no response, or at least an inadequate response, to insist that all critical matters of individual liberty should *not* be left to public debate. That is exactly where such matters must *begin*. The Declaration reminds us that we are a people, and the only "just" laws enacted by our government are those that have been *consented* to by the people. The American people have consented to a government neither wholly national nor wholly federal and under which the most essential aspects of human freedom are first discussed in homes, churches, town squares, legislative chambers, and—ultimately—the halls of Congress.

To date, the American people have proved themselves worthy of their Declaration. The movement to abolish slavery emerged alongside the movement for American independence. The people's vote achieved the aims of abolitionism in 1865. The people also included the rights of life, liberty, and the pursuit of happiness in their original Bill of Rights, and they expanded access to those rights when they voted to ratify the 14th Amendment in 1868.

The same federalist structure that facilitated the democratic advance of liberty in the past continues to do so today. The dynamic tension between freedom and federalism lives on in debates over immigration, sanctuary cities, abortion, biological sex, climate change, and a host of other issues relating to personal and political freedom. Here's to the next 250 years of American liberty.

Notes

1. G. Edward White, *Law in American History*, vol. 1, *From the Colonial Years Through the Civil War* (Oxford University Press, 2012), 397. See also Pekka Hämäläinen, *The Comanche Empire* (Yale University Press, 2009); and William S. Kiser, *Borderlands of Slavery: The Struggle over Captivity and Peonage in the American Southwest* (University of Pennsylvania Press, 2021), 1.

2. Kiser, *Borderlands of Slavery*.

3. See, for example, "Virginia Slave Code (1705)," in *The Reconstruction Amendments: The Essential Documents*, ed. Kurt T. Lash, vol. 1 (University of Chicago Press, 2021). See also Sean Wilentz, *No Property in Man: Slavery and Antislavery at the Nation's Founding* (Harvard University Press, 2018), 27.

4. Wilentz, *No Property in Man*, 25. This organization continued after the Revolution and eventually elected Benjamin Franklin as its president. See Edward Needles, *An Historical Memoir of the Pennsylvania Society: For Promoting the Abolition of Slavery; The Relief of Free Negroes Unlawfully Held in Bondage, and for Improving the Condition of the African Race* (Merrihew & Thompson, 1848), 29.

5. See "1777 Constitution of Vermont," in *The Federal and State Constitutions, Colonial Charters, and Other Organic Laws of the States, Territories, and Colonies Now or Heretofore Forming the United States of America*, ed. Francis Newton Thorpe, vol. 5, *New Jersey—Philippine Islands* (Government Printing Office, 1909), 3739.

6. Wilentz, *No Property in Man*, 5.

7. Wilentz, *No Property in Man*, 5. Vermont officially became a state in 1791.

8. See "The Northwest Ordinance (July 13, 1787)," in Lash, *The Reconstruction Amendments*, 1:10.

9. Paul Finkelman, *Slavery and the Founders: Race and Liberty in the Age of Jefferson*, 3rd ed. (Routledge, 2014), 34.

10. The territory eventually became the states of Illinois, Indiana, Michigan, Minnesota, Ohio, and Wisconsin.

11. US Const. pmbl.

12. *Federalist*, no. 45 (James Madison). "Publius" was the common pseudonym used by the papers' three authors, James Madison, Alexander Hamilton, and John Jay.

13. US Const. art. IV.

14. "Debates in the Philadelphia Constitutional Convention (June, July, Aug. 1787)," in Lash, *The Reconstruction Amendments*, 1:184.

15. See US Const. amend. IX ("The enumeration in the constitution of certain rights shall not be construed to deny or disparage other rights retained by the people.").

16. See US Const. amend. X ("The powers not delegated to the United States by the Constitution, nor prohibited by it to the States, are reserved to the States respectively, or to the people.").

17. *Federalist*, no. 39 (James Madison).

18. See generally *Federalist*, no. 51 (James Madison).

19. See *Federalist*, no. 46 (James Madison).

20. *Federalist*, no. 44 (James Madison).

21. See "The Alien and Sedition Acts (July 6, July 14, 1798)," in Lash, *The Reconstruction Amendments*, 1:36.

22. "The Alien and Sedition Acts (July 6, July 14, 1798)," in Lash, *The Reconstruction Amendments*.

23. See "The Kentucky Resolutions of 1798 (Nov. 10, 1798)," in Lash, *The Reconstruction Amendments*, 1:37; and "The Virginia Resolutions (Dec. 24, 1798)," in Lash, *The Reconstruction Amendments*, 1:38.

24. See "James Madison, Report on the Virginia Resolutions," in Lash, *The Reconstruction Amendments*, 1:41, 51.

25. "James Madison, Report on the Virginia Resolutions (Jan. 7, 1800)," in Lash, *The Reconstruction Amendments*, 1:42.

26. See Dred Scott v. Sandford, 60 US 393 (1857).

27. See Jack N. Rakove, ed., *James Madison: Writings* (Library of America, 1999), 608.

28. See Ralph Ketcham, *James Madison: A Biography* (University of Virginia Press, 1990), 406.

29. Madison's "Report of 1800" and the Federalist Papers dominated American political rhetoric in the early 19th century. See Kurt T. Lash, "James Madison's Celebrated Report of 1800: The Transformation of the Tenth Amendment," *George Washington Law Review* 74, no. 165 (2006); and Kurt T. Lash, "The Federalist and the Fourteenth Amendment—Publius in Antebellum Public Debate, 1788–1860," *Brigham*

Young University Law Review 48, no. 6 (2023): 1831. Meanwhile, the first American constitutional treatise, St. George Tucker's *View of the Constitution of the United States*, expressly relied on the Federalist Papers, the Virginia Resolutions, and Madison's Report. See, for example, "St. George Tucker, *A View of the Constitution* (1803)," in Lash, *The Reconstruction Amendments*, 1:63–64, 74–75.

30. US Const. art. IV, § 2, cl. 3.

31. "Fugitive Slave Act (Feb. 12, 1793)," in Lash, *The Reconstruction Amendments*, 1:188.

32. "Fugitive Slave Act (Feb. 12, 1793)," in Lash, *The Reconstruction Amendments*.

33. See Prigg v. Pennsylvania, 41 US 550 (1842), which references "an Act to give effect to the provisions of the constitution of the United States relative to fugitives from labor, for the protection of free people of color, and to prevent Kidnapping."

34. See Wilentz, *No Property in Man*, 226.

35. *Prigg*, 41 US at 539.

36. *Prigg*, 41 US at 542.

37. For examples of this resistance and its religious motivation, see Stephanie H. Barclay and Kurt T. Lash, "A Crust of Bread: Religious Resistance and the Fourteenth Amendment," *Vanderbilt Law Review* 71, no. 4 (2025): 1203–64.

38. Ten of the first 12 presidents owned slaves (John Adams and John Quincy Adams being the exceptions), and every president before Lincoln enforced the Fugitive Slave Acts.

39. See "US House of Representatives, the 'Gag' Rules, (May 26, 1836)," in Lash, *The Reconstruction Amendments*, 1:216.

40. See "Letter of Postmaster General Amos Kendall Regarding the Delivery of Anti-Slavery Literature, *Richmond Whig* (Aug. 11, 1835)," in Lash, *The Reconstruction Amendments*, 1:210.

41. See 10 Stat. 277 (1854).

42. *Dred Scott*, 60 US at 393.

43. See, for example, "Wendell Phillips, *The Constitution: A Pro-Slavery Compact* (1844)," in Lash, *The Reconstruction Amendments*, 1:227; and "'No Union with Slaveholders,' *Liberator* (July 7, 1854)," in Lash, *The Reconstruction Amendments*, 1:259.

44. See Randy E. Barnett, "Whence Comes Section One? The Abolitionist Origins of the Fourteenth Amendment," *Journal of Legal Analysis* 3, no. 1 (2011): 165.

45. "Liberty Party Platform (Aug. 30, 1843)," in Lash, *The Reconstruction Amendments*, 1:225.

46. "Free Soil Party Platform (Aug. 9–10, 1848)," in Lash, *The Reconstruction Amendments*, 1:236.

47. "Republican Party Platform (May 17, 1860)," in Lash, *The Reconstruction Amendments*, 1:320.

48. See "US Congress, the 'Corwin Amendment' (Mar. 2, 1861)," in Lash, *The Reconstruction Amendments*, 1:343.

49. "Abraham Lincoln, First Inaugural Address (Mar. 4, 1861)," in Lash, *The Reconstruction Amendments*, 1:347.

50. See, for example, "South Carolina, Declaration of the Causes Which Justify Secession (Dec. 24, 1860)," in Lash, *The Reconstruction Amendments*, 1:327.

51. See, for example, "John C. Calhoun, *A Discourse on the Constitution* (I)(1851)," in Lash, *The Reconstruction Amendments*, 1:144.

52. See, for example, "South Carolina, Declaration of the Causes Which Justify Secession (Dec. 24, 1860)," in Lash, *The Reconstruction Amendments*, 1:328. The protection of slavery through provisions like the fugitive slave clause "was so material to the compact, that without it the compact would not have been made."

53. See James M. McPherson, *Battle Cry of Freedom: The Civil War Era* (Oxford University Press, 1988), 771.

54. The fall of Atlanta to Union forces in early September 1864 was particularly important. For a discussion of the battle for Atlanta and its political significance, see McPherson, *Battle Cry of Freedom*, 774.

55. For a general discussion of the amendment's drafting and passage, see Kurt T. Lash, "Introduction to Part 2A," in *The Reconstruction Amendments*, 1:373.

56. "The Northwest Ordinance (July 13, 1787)," in Lash, *The Reconstruction Amendments*, 1:10.

57. US Const. amend. XIII (1865); and "The Northwest Ordinance (July 13, 1787)," in Lash, *The Reconstruction Amendments*, 1:10.

58. See, for example, "Liberty Party Platform (Aug. 30, 1843)," in Lash, *The Reconstruction Amendments*, 1:225. "RESOLVED, That the fundamental truths of the Declaration of Independence, that all men are endowed by their Creator with certain inalienable rights, among which are life, liberty, and the pursuit of happiness, was made the fundamental law of our national government, by that amendment of the constitution which declares that no person shall be deprived of life, liberty, or property, without due process of law."

59. See Kurt T. Lash, "The State Citizenship Clause," *University of Pennsylvania Journal of Constitutional Law* 25, no. 5 (2023): 1097, 1147, https://scholarship.law.upenn.edu/cgi/viewcontent.cgi?article=1863&context=jcl.

60. US National Archives, "14th Amendment to the U.S. Constitution: Civil Rights (1868)," https://www.archives.gov/milestone-documents/14th-amendment.

61. Abraham Lincoln, "Fragment on the Constitution and the Union," ca. January 1861, in *The Collected Works of Abraham Lincoln*, ed. Roy P. Basler, vol. 4, *1860–1861* (Rutgers University Press, 1953), 169.

62. See "John C. Calhoun, *A Discourse on the Constitution* (I) (1851)," in Lash, *The Reconstruction Amendments*, 1:142. Madison himself rejected the idea of state secession and its only slightly less radical sibling, state nullification. See "James Madison to Daniel Webster (Mar. 15, 1833)," in Lash, *The Reconstruction Amendments*, 1:115.

63. See Lash, "The Federalist and the Fourteenth Amendment."

64. Texas v. White, 74 US 700, 725 (1869).

65. See Cong. Globe, 37th Cong., 2nd Sess. 737 (1862). According to Sumner: "Any votes of secession or other act by which any State may undertake to put an end to the

supremacy of the Constitution within its territory is inoperative and void against the Constitution, and when sustained by force it becomes a practical *abdication* by the State of all rights under the Constitution, while the treason which it involves still further works an instant *forfeiture* of all those functions and powers essential to the continued existence of the State as a body politic, so that from that time forward the territory falls under the exclusive jurisdiction of Congress as other territory, and the State being, according to the language of the law, *felo-de-se*, ceases to exist."

66. In the opening days of the 38th Congress, for example, Representative Lovejoy proposed "a bill to give effect to the Declaration of Independence" and the Fifth Amendment's due process clause, which would abolish slavery throughout the United States. See "US House of Representatives, Proposed Abolition Amendments (Ashley Wilson) and Abolition Bill (Lovejoy) (Dec. 14, 1863)," in Lash, *The Reconstruction Amendments*, 1:385.

67. John A. Bingham, *One Country, One Constitution, and One People* [. . .] (Congressional Globe Office, 1866), 7.

68. Bingham, *One Country, One Constitution, and One People*.

69. Bingham, *One Country, One Constitution, and One People*.

70. Cong. Globe, 39th Cong., 2nd Sess. 250–51 (1867).

71. Cong. Globe, 39th Cong., 2nd Sess. 504 (1867).

72. Civil Rights Cases, 109 US 3, 20–21 (1883).

73. See Brown v. Board of Education of Topeka, 347 US 483 (1954); Parents Involved in Community Schools v. Seattle School District No. 1, 551 US 701 (2007); and Students for Fair Admissions v. University of North Carolina, 600 US ___ (2023).

74. New York v. United States, 505 US 144 (1992); and United States v. Lopez, 514 US 549 (1995).

75. Bond v. United States, 564 US 211 (2011).

76. *Bond*, 564 US at 8–9.

77. *Federalist*, no. 45 (Madison).

78. Kurt T. Lash, "Becoming the 'Bill of Rights': The First Ten Amendments from Founding to Reconstruction," *Virginia Law Review* 110, no. 2 (2024): 474–75. For an explanation of how the 14th Amendment incorporates all of the Bill of Rights, including the 10th Amendment, see Kurt T. Lash, *The Fourteenth Amendment and the Privileges and Immunities of American Citizenship* (Cambridge University Press, 2014).

79. "In the compound republic of America, the power surrendered by the people is first divided between two distinct governments, and then the portion allotted to each subdivided among distinct and separate departments. Hence a double security arises to the rights of the people." *Federalist*, no. 51 (Madison).

80. James Hershman, "Massive Resistance," *Encyclopedia Virginia*, December 7, 2020, https://encyclopediavirginia.org/entries/massive-resistance/.

81. James Madison, "Notes on Nullification, December 1834," Founders Online, https://founders.archives.gov/documents/Madison/99-02-02-3190.

3

Lincoln's Battle for the Founders' Declaration

LUCAS E. MOREL

A braham Lincoln once said that public opinion "always has a '*central idea*,' from which all its minor thoughts radiate." He thought that in America, that idea "at the beginning was, and until recently has continued to be, 'the equality of men.'" He made that comment in December 1856, following the defeat of the Republican Party's first candidate for president, John C. Frémont. Given that the Democratic candidate, James Buchanan, won with barely 45 percent of the popular vote in a three-man race that also included former Whig President Millard Fillmore, Lincoln remained hopeful that the founding principle of equality would regain its political sway. Buchanan's election, Lincoln argued, "was a struggle, by one party, to discard that central idea, and to substitute for it the opposite idea that slavery is right." If not opposed, he believed it would produce "the perpetuity of human slavery, and its extension to all countries and colors" rather than the "steady progress towards the practical equality of all men" that had marked the development of American self-government.[1] Over the next four years, Lincoln would battle rhetorically for the mantle of the American founders, seeking to reclaim human equality as the central idea of the American Revolution.

Not all Americans defined equality the same way. Believing that dealing with slavery correctly depended on defining equality correctly, Lincoln found guidance by turning to the American founders. There was no greater influence on Lincoln's statesmanship than the leading men and the leading ideas of the American Revolution and the nation's constitutional formation.

But weren't the founders slaveholders and therefore racists? What kind of help can that old generation provide modern-day Americans? Lincoln saw in the American Revolution a people forged in the crucible of British resistance to their attempt to rule themselves. In that process, they established principles and institutions based on human equality, individual rights, and government by consent of the governed. To be sure, in the midst of fighting for their right to govern themselves, they did not abolish slavery right away. Lincoln argued that when Americans fought for independence and then framed the Constitution, they were "in a certain sense compelled to tolerate" slavery. "It was a sort of necessity."[2] However, they viewed it as "an evil not to be extended"[3] and within the federal system sought "the peaceful extinction of slavery."[4] As Lincoln explained in 1858,

> I think that was the condition in which we found ourselves when we established this government. We had slavery among us, we could not get our Constitution unless we permitted them to remain in slavery, we could not secure the good we did secure if we grasped for more, and having by necessity submitted to that much, it does not destroy the principle that is the charter of our liberties.[5]

That charter was what Lincoln called "that old Declaration of Independence," from which he consistently quoted its statement "that all men are created equal." To lose sight of this principle would "tend to rub out the sentiment of liberty in the country," Lincoln warned, and would "transform this Government into a government of some other form."[6]

The idea of getting right with the founders was not unique to Lincoln. In fact, the two main alternatives to the Republican Party during the pivotal 1860 presidential campaign and the ensuing secession winter each appealed to the American founders to support their respective policies. Northern Democrats supported Lincoln's longtime rival, Illinois Senator Stephen A. Douglas. He argued that "our Revolutionary fathers" were unconcerned about the future of slavery in America. Douglas claimed the founders endorsed what he called "Popular Sovereignty."[7] As he declared in his first formal debate with Lincoln in 1858, "Our fathers intended that our institutions should differ," adding that "Washington, Jefferson, Franklin, Madison, Hamilton, Jay, and the great men of that day, made this Government divided into free States and slave States, and left each State perfectly free to do as it pleased on the subject of slavery."[8] Douglas touted this policy as a form of "diversity":

> The fathers of the Revolution, and the sages who made the Constitution, . . . well understood that the great varieties of soil, of production and of interests, in a Republic as large as this, required different local and domestic regulations in each locality, adapted to the wants and interests of each separate State.[9]

On the other hand, "uniformity in local and domestic affairs would be destructive of State rights, of State sovereignty, of personal liberty and personal freedom. Uniformity is the parent of despotism the world over, not only in politics, but in religion." Douglas argued that Lincoln sought "one consolidated empire" in his insistence on racial equality.[10]

A month after Southern Democrats split from their Northern counterparts and nominated sitting Vice President John C. Breckinridge of Kentucky as their presidential candidate, Breckinridge said, "The Government our fathers gave us" enshrined "equality of the States of the Union" as "the great fundamental principle" of the Constitution. "That Constitution," he continued, "was framed and transmitted by the wisest generation of men that ever lived." Moreover, "the principles upon which it was originally framed" comprised not only state equality but also "equality of the rights of the citizens in their persons and property," which included property in slaves.[11] In a September 1860 campaign speech, Breckinridge argued that "the common Territories of the Union" were "open to the common settlement from all the States," insisting on the right of Southern slave owners to settle in federal territory with their slaves.[12] The first plank of the Southern Democratic Party platform reinforced this view, stating, "All citizens of the United States have an equal right to settle with their property in the Territory, without their rights, either of person or property, being destroyed or impaired by congressional or territorial legislation."[13]

Adhering to Chief Justice Roger Taney's notorious 1857 opinion in *Dred Scott v. Sandford*, Breckinridge claimed that "between slave property and other property, no distinction exists." Therefore, Congress has "the power, coupled with the duty, of guarding and protecting the owner in his rights" in federal territory.[14] Although the speech was designed to get Douglas to withdraw from the presidential race, Breckinridge did not forget the Republican candidate. He said Lincoln "represents the most obnoxious principles in issue in this canvass." Breckinridge claimed that these principles were "clearly unconstitutional" because they disregarded Taney's ruling in *Dred Scott*, which interpreted the Fifth Amendment's due process clause to guarantee a federal right to property, including slaves.[15]

Southern Democrats had rejected Douglas as their party's nominee for president because he would not endorse a federal law guaranteeing the right to enslave black people in the territories. They eventually tried to secede from the United States and drew language from the Declaration to justify their attempt to form an independent Southern nation. They even modeled their Confederate Constitution after the United States Constitution, with the distinction that the former contained explicit guarantees of "the right of property in negro slaves."[16] James Thornwell, a slave-owning preacher from South Carolina, insisted that secessionists were "upholding the great principles which our fathers bequeathed" and "the very liberty for which Washington bled, and which the heroes of the Revolution achieved."[17]

And so the election of 1860 was essentially a referendum on *whose* interpretation of the American founding was correct. Near the start of that election year, Lincoln exhorted Americans to "HAVE FAITH THAT RIGHT MAKES MIGHT." He defended the Republicans as the founding's true heirs because of their commitment to stopping the spread of slavery:

> As those fathers marked it, so let it be again marked, as an evil not
> to be extended, but to be tolerated and protected only because of and

so far as its actual presence among us makes that toleration and protection a necessity.[18]

Lincoln believed that during his contentious times, looking back to the founding could actually help Americans move forward. He did this most famously in his 1863 Gettysburg Address. That speech opens at the nation's beginning: "Four score and seven years ago our fathers brought forth on this continent, a new nation, conceived in Liberty, and dedicated to the proposition that all men are created equal."[19] Lincoln takes his audience back not to the Constitution but to the Declaration—not to the body but to the soul of the nation.

The Original Idea

Lincoln delivered his Gettysburg remarks in the Year of Jubilee, the year of the Emancipation Proclamation. Union soldiers and sailors were now charged by the president to protect the freedom of liberated former slaves in the rebelling states. In his speech, Lincoln did not announce a new principle of freedom but affirmed an old one—one he learned from the founders when they declared independence. What Lincoln called at Gettysburg "a new birth of freedom" was directly tied to the old, original birth of freedom, our *first* emancipation proclamation—the Declaration of Independence. Its central idea that "all men are created equal" described the equal possession of rights by every human being. Lincoln spoke on the battlefield of "the unfinished work" to which all living Americans could dedicate themselves. The survival of "government of the people, by the people, for the people" would now benefit over three million newly freed black men and women. By defending the Union and its founding vision of human equality, Americans could honor the men who fought and died at Gettysburg— those "who here gave their lives that that nation might live."[20]

Lincoln went on to explain that the Civil War was a test of America's purpose: as he put it, "whether that nation, or any nation so conceived and so dedicated, can long endure."[21] With Americans shooting not at a foreign enemy but at each other, clearly there was some confusion about the meaning of America. This is why as president-elect, Lincoln called Americans God's "*almost* chosen people."[22] (Emphasis added.) He believed Americans were undergoing an identity crisis, divided as they were in their understanding of why the nation existed and over its highest aims and purposes. Lincoln thought the nation would benefit from looking to its past. Americans needed a reminder of why the nation was founded in the first place and therefore why the union of American states was worth saving.

This was no Civil War epiphany of Lincoln's. In February 1861, as he headed to the nation's capital to be inaugurated as president, he stopped in Trenton, the capital of New Jersey, and told the state senate, "I am exceedingly anxious that this Union, the Constitution, and the liberties of the people shall be perpetuated in accordance with the original idea for which that struggle was made."[23] A nation devoted to the principle of human equality needed to endure.

In the decade leading up to the 1860 presidential election, Lincoln's appeal to the American founding was not directed at slave-owning *Southerners*. They had long rejected the view that slavery was a necessary evil. Lincoln's main concern was that white *Northerners* would be tempted by Douglas's theory of popular sovereignty because it was neutral on the slave question. In reference to the enslavement of black people out West, Douglas said, "I don't care whether it be voted up or down."[24] He did not think his position as a United States senator should have any influence, let alone any authority, over whether slavery was permitted in the federal territories. Douglas believed that whites at the local level had the right to decide the question without interference from Congress.

However, Douglas's definition of popular sovereignty implied that slavery's expansion or restriction in the United States would be determined not by a majority of all American citizens but by a very small majority of those who settled in the Western territories. This indicated to Lincoln that the greatest obstacle to stopping the spread of slavery in the United States was Douglas persuading white Northerners to join him in ignoring the plight of black people in the federal territories. As Lincoln put it:

> They tell us that they desire the people of a territory to vote slavery out or in as they please. . . . The question arises, "slavery or freedom?" Caring nothing about it, they let it come in, and that is the end of it. It is the surest way of nationalizing the institution. Just as certain, but more dangerous because more insidious; but it is leading us there just as certainly and as surely as Jeff. Davis himself would have us go.[25]

What made Douglas's "don't care" policy so "insidious" was that for slavery to become nationalized, no politician *north* of the Mason–Dixon line needed to argue in its favor. Simply getting white Americans *in the free states* not to care whether the enslavement of black people became legal in federal territory sufficed. Once slavery was accepted as a constitutional right in the territories, it would soon become a federal right in the free states regardless of what their laws or constitutions said. If white Northerners agreed with Douglas that Congress did not have authority to regulate the domestic institutions of the territories, then Douglas's "*declared* indifference" would actually represent, in Lincoln's words, "covert *real* zeal for the spread of slavery."[26]

Lincoln therefore called on Americans as early as 1854 to "re-adopt the Declaration of Independence." In so doing, they would "not only have saved the Union" but in his words "so saved it, as to make, and to keep it, forever worthy of the saving."[27] Americans needed to follow the example of the founders, who banned slavery in the Northwest Territory—first under the Articles of Confederation and then under the Constitution. A country worthy of saving needed to be a country that limited the spread of slavery as a first step to securing its eventual demise.

A Standard Maxim

A year after the *Dred Scott* decision, stopping the spread of slavery in the United States became the focus of Lincoln's 1858 Senate campaign against the incumbent, Douglas. Lincoln advanced a pro-freedom interpretation of the American founding to counter alternative interpretations promoted by influential figures such as Taney and Douglas. Unlike Lincoln, Taney and Douglas thought the Declaration of Independence's principles were true only for white people. They read the Declaration that way to defend the slaveholding founders from charges of hypocrisy. In his 1857 *Dred Scott* opinion, Taney wrote,

> The enslaved African race were not intended to be included, and formed no part of the people who framed and adopted this declaration; for if the language, as understood in that day, would embrace them, the conduct of the distinguished men who framed the Declaration of Independence would have been utterly and flagrantly inconsistent with the principles they asserted.[28]

Douglas echoed this reading of the Declaration a year later during his debates with Lincoln in Illinois:

> Are you willing to have it said—that every man who signed the Declaration of Independence declared the negro his equal, and then was hypocrite enough to continue to hold him as a slave, in violation of what he believed to be the divine law? And yet when you say that the Declaration of Independence includes the negro, you charge the signers of it with hypocrisy.[29]

Douglas inferred, plausibly enough, that if Lincoln's reading black people into the Declaration was correct, the founders were bound, as conscientious men, that day and that hour, not only to have abolished slavery throughout the land, but to have conferred political rights and privileges on the negro, and elevated him to an equality with the white man.[30]

He then contended that their decision not to free their slaves "shows that they did not understand the language they used [in the Declaration] to include any but the white race."[31]

The social context shaped how Lincoln and Douglas appealed to the Illinois citizenry. White supremacy was not the exception but the rule in the free state of Illinois. The few blacks who resided in that state possessed few civil rights and no political rights. According to the 1848 constitution, only white males could vote or serve in the state militia.[32] Illinois statutes barred blacks from serving on juries and offering testimony against whites in courts.[33] In 1853, as authorized by the 1848 constitution, the state legislature passed an act "to prevent the immigration of free Negroes into this state."[34] Douglas routinely exploited the racial animus of white Illinoisans by calling Lincoln's political party the "Black Republican party" or "Abolition party."[35]

Lincoln responded by tying the future security of the rights of white people to the present insecurity of the rights of black people. Given the color prejudice of most white Illinoisans and given that no blacks were allowed to vote in 1858, it is extraordinary that Lincoln kept bringing up the natural rights of blacks during the debates and explicitly reading the black man into, not out of, the Declaration. Even when he appealed to the self-interest of bigoted white Illinoisans, he never did so without showing them the true basis of their rights—namely, the Declaration's principle of human equality. In this way, he hoped white prejudice would eventually yield to claims of common humanity regardless of color.

In his critique of Taney's *Dred Scott* ruling, Lincoln elaborated on the meaning of equality in the Declaration. He said the founders

did not mean to assert the obvious untruth, that all were then actually enjoying that equality, nor yet, that they were about to confer it immediately upon them. In fact they had no power to confer such a boon. They meant simply to declare the *right,* so that the *enforcement* of it might follow as fast as circumstances should permit.[36]

Lincoln understood the founders not as hypocritical politicians but as prudent revolutionaries. They recognized that in addition to long-standing prejudice and economic self-interest, circumstances like a war with Great Britain and a potential war between the races would prevent immediate and mass emancipation in any state, especially those with a significant slave population.

Simply put, at the time of the founding, Americans did not believe they could free both themselves and their slaves. To do so would jeopardize their efforts to secure and maintain their independence from England. The success of the American Revolution would require a united effort by the American states, a unity the states continued to see as essential once independence was achieved. Lincoln believed that to establish a viable government—"to form a more perfect Union," as the Constitution notes in its preamble[37]—the founders had to make compromises. In their minds, liberty required independence, independence required unity, and unity required allowing slavery to survive in the states where it already existed.

Lincoln also observed that the founders' inaction regarding enslaved *blacks* in America was similar to their inaction toward free *whites.* While it was obvious that equality was not secured for black people on American soil, Lincoln pointed out the less obvious fact that the founders "did not at once, *or ever afterwards,* actually place all white people on an equality with one another."[38] For example, in the early decades following American independence, states employed property and religious qualifications to limit the right to vote.[39] This meant that not all white people were made equal in their civil or political rights. Equality as a political reality would come by fits and starts, even for white Americans. Lincoln surmised that the Declaration set up a standard maxim for free society, which should be familiar to all, and revered by all; constantly looked to, constantly labored for, . . . and thereby constantly spreading and deepening its influence, and augmenting the happiness and value of life to all people of all colors everywhere.[40]

While natural rights were the birthright of every person, the vesting of civil and political rights would depend on the political sentiments of a given community. Lincoln strove to keep equality in the forefront of the public mind so that it would continue to inspire Americans to bring it to political fruition.

Between the Kansas-Nebraska Act of 1854, which Douglas helped pass, and the *Dred Scott* decision, Lincoln believed the expansion of slavery was gaining ground. As he warned in his "House Divided" speech in June 1858,

> Another Supreme Court decision, declaring that the Constitution of the United States does not permit a *state* to exclude slavery from its limits . . .
>
> . . . is all that slavery now lacks of being alike lawful in all the States. . . .
>
> . . . We shall *lie down* pleasantly dreaming that the people of *Missouri* are on the verge of making their State *free*; and we shall *awake* to the *reality*, instead, that the *Supreme* Court has made *Illinois* a *slave* State.[41]

What Lincoln and the founders called a "self-evident" truth—"that all men are created equal"—Douglas called "a monstrous heresy."[42] Douglas would eventually appeal to white supremacy as a Union-saving measure after Lincoln's surprising election to the presidency in 1860—an election that provoked South Carolina to dissolve its union with the rest of the American states. To his credit, Douglas remained a staunch unionist. But he thought the way to keep slaveholding states from following South Carolina was by writing the color line into the Constitution.

On December 24, 1860, Douglas proposed two constitutional amendments. A 13th Amendment would block Congress from making any laws regarding slavery in the territories. His proposed 14th Amendment stated: "The elective franchise and the right to hold office, whether federal, State, territorial, or municipal, shall not be exercised by persons of the African race, in whole or in part."[43] The contrast between Douglas's 14th Amendment and the one that passed during Reconstruction could not be more striking. Where the later 14th Amendment speaks of "the equal protection of the laws,"[44] Douglas sought a constitutional ban against black Americans voting or holding political office at any level throughout the United States. If anything distinguishes Lincoln's approach to the problem of slavery in America from Douglas's, it is Lincoln's consistent attempt to get white Americans to acknowledge what they had in common with black Americans—the equal possession of natural rights.

The Apple of Gold

A year before he was first elected president, Lincoln was invited to speak in Boston to mark the anniversary of Thomas Jefferson's birth. Since he couldn't make the trip, he sent a letter extolling Jefferson's achievement in drafting the Declaration of Independence. He wrote that "the principles of Jefferson are the definitions and axioms of free society."[45] Lincoln drew from his study of Euclid's geometry to picture the Declaration's principles as the building blocks of democracy. But Lincoln acknowledged that even self-evident truths can be "denied, and evaded," as tolerance of Southern slavery demonstrated in 1859. Nevertheless, he insisted: "This is a world of compensations; and he who would be no slave, must consent to have no slave."[46] Alluding to Jefferson's critique of slavery in *Notes on the State of Virginia*, Lincoln added that "those who deny freedom to others, deserve it not for themselves; and, under a just God, can not long retain it."[47]

These were astounding words for Lincoln the Republican and former Whig to utter, given the success that states' rights Democrats achieved in donning the mantle of Jefferson, one of the founders of the Democratic Party. Still, Lincoln declared:

> All honor to Jefferson—to the man who, in the concrete pressure of a struggle for national independence by a single people, had the coolness, forecast, and capacity to introduce into a merely revolutionary document, an abstract truth, applicable to all men and all times, and so to embalm it there, that to-day, and in all coming days, it shall be a rebuke and a stumbling-block to the very harbingers of re-appearing tyranny and oppression.[48]

In celebrating Jefferson, Lincoln looked back to a founding generation that put the principles of self-government in writing—principles that he invited fellow citizens to recognize as the true source of their rights and that obligated them to eliminate slavery as fast as circumstances should permit.

After Lincoln's election in the fall of 1860, he received a letter from Alexander Stephens, a Georgia Democrat, who had been a Whig colleague of Lincoln's during Lincoln's one term in Congress, in the late 1840s. Before Georgia's secession from the Union, Stephens wrote in December 1860 asking Lincoln to speak to the nation before his March 4 inauguration "to save our common country." Quoting Proverbs 25, Stephens suggested to Lincoln that "a word fitly spoken by you now would be like 'apples of gold in pictures of silver.'"[49]

Lincoln mulled over that Bible verse and jotted a note to himself—a reflection on what he called the "philosophical cause" of American prosperity. He had long revered the Constitution and saw the union of the American states as essential to the republic's success. "Even these, are not the primary cause of our great prosperity," Lincoln wrote.

> There is something back of these, entwining itself more closely about the human heart. That something, is the principle of

"Liberty to all"—the principle that clears the *path* for all—gives *hope* to all—and, by consequence, *enterprize*, and *industry* to all.[50]

Lincoln then alluded to the line from Proverbs that Stephens had cited, but focused on the principle of "Liberty to all":

The assertion of that *principle*, at *that time*, was *the* word, *"fitly spoken"* which has proved an "apple of gold" to us. The *Union*, and the *Constitution*, are the *picture* of *silver*, subsequently framed around it. The picture was made, not to *conceal*, or *destroy* the apple; but to *adorn*, and *preserve* it. The *picture* was made for the apple—*not* the apple for the picture.[51]

Contrary to what Stephens wanted from Lincoln, what the country needed was not a new word from its new president but old words from fathers of old expressed in the Declaration. Lincoln saw the Declaration's principle of "Liberty to all"—the equal rights possessed by all human beings—as the moral compass of the Constitution and the union of American states, even if it had been misinterpreted or broken in defense of the right to enslave human beings.

By the time Lincoln was inaugurated president, on March 4, 1861, seven slaveholding states had declared their "secession" from the American union and formed a confederation whose constitution protected "the right of property in negro slaves."[52] Despite having argued against Georgia's secession, Stephens was elected vice president of the Confederate States of America. On March 21, 1861, he argued that the new Confederate Constitution was an improvement over the old one Lincoln was trying to preserve. It was better not simply because it protected slavery by mentioning it explicitly, where the original Constitution never even used the word. There were plenty of countries throughout history that practiced slavery. But Stephens argued that the Confederacy had distinguished itself by being the first to base its slave society on white supremacy.

What set Stephens apart from most Confederates was his view that the American founders believed "that the enslavement of the African was in violation of the laws of nature; that it was wrong in principle, socially, morally, and politically."[53] Here he fully agreed with Lincoln's understanding of the founders. However, Stephens differed from Lincoln by arguing that the Confederate Constitution was better than the founders' Constitution because it was

> founded upon exactly the opposite idea; its foundations are laid, its corner-stone rests, upon the great truth that the negro is not equal to the white man; that slavery subordination to the superior race is his natural and normal condition.[54]

His was a categorical rejection of the founders' declaration that all men are created equal. Stephens proclaimed, "This, our new government, is the first, in the history of the world, based upon this great physical, philosophical, and moral truth." Stephens argued that the antislavery principles of the founding "were fundamentally wrong. They rested upon the assumption of the equality of races." Founding the American republic on human equality was "an error" and "a sandy foundation," unlike the new and improved constitution he helped draft for the Confederate States of America. To demonstrate the superiority of the Confederate Constitution over the United States Constitution, Stephens looked back to the founders to reject their claim about the equality of all human beings.[55]

In contrast, Lincoln turned to the founders to affirm human equality as the only legitimate basis for self-government. But that very equality imposed on Americans a moral obligation to abolish slavery in a manner consistent with the consent that was the flip side of equality's coin. For government simply to "do the right thing" by exercising powers not delegated to it by the governed would violate the consent of the people. Lincoln's respect for the consent of the governed, what he called "the sheet anchor of American republicanism,"[56] governed his approach to emancipation. As he put it late in the Civil War,

If slavery is not wrong, nothing is wrong. I can not remember when I did not so think, and feel. And yet I have never understood that the Presidency conferred upon me an unrestricted right to act officially upon this judgment and feeling."[57]

Lincoln believed that a government based on consent could not act simply according to personal conviction and moral principle; it could only do so under duly granted constitutional authority.

He made the distinction between "*official* duty" and "*personal* wish" most famously in a letter to *New-York Tribune* editor Horace Greeley published in August 1862. With a draft of the Emancipation Proclamation already written and shared with only his cabinet the month prior, Lincoln said to Greeley:

My paramount object in this struggle *is* to save the Union, and is *not* either to save or to destroy slavery. If I could save the Union without freeing *any* slave I would do it, and if I could save it by freeing *all* the slaves I would do it; and if I could save it by freeing some and leaving others alone I would also do that.[58]

Because emancipation remained controversial as an exercise of federal power, Lincoln tied it to the noncontroversial end of saving the Union. He would eventually justify his presidential proclamation in his role as commander in chief "in time of actual armed rebellion,"[59] buttressed by Congress's Confiscation Act of July 17, 1862.

As president, Lincoln turned a humanitarian end—the liberation of enslaved black Americans—into a constitutional means, "a fit and necessary war measure for suppressing said rebellion," as he put it in his Emancipation Proclamation.[60] Or, as Frederick Douglass observed, "The slaves' liberation is the country's salvation."[61] In this way, the liberation of chattel slaves by the president of the United States would be not only "an act of justice" but also "warranted by the Constitution, upon military necessity."[62] By finding a constitutional way to liberate slaves, Lincoln sought to make both his means and his ends a faithful expression of the consent of the American people on behalf of human equality.

Worthy of Saving

Lincoln's campaign for president in 1860 was the culmination of efforts begun in 1854 to teach the American people the true basis of their rights and the constitutional path to the abolition of slavery. His speeches as a citizen and president, as well as actions that both saved the Union and emancipated slaves, were the primary reason white supremacy did not become a "systemic" part of American self-government at the national level.

By electing and then reelecting Lincoln and his interpretation of the Declaration of Independence, the American people rejected both the "positive good" argument for the enslavement of black people and the toleration of the spread of racial slavery under the auspices of Douglas's popular sovereignty. Lincoln understood the Declaration as enshrining the principle of human equality, "an abstract truth, applicable to all men and all times."[63] He referred to it as "the 'equality of man' principle" and believed that it "actuated our forefathers in the establishment of the government" and "that slavery, being directly opposed to this, is morally wrong."[64]

As a student of the American founding, Lincoln became its greatest defender. He not only fought—and fought successfully—to preserve the American union but also explained in words yet to be surpassed why America was "worthy of the saving." By reclaiming equality as the central idea of the nation's birth and key driver of American social and political progress, Lincoln helped Americans recover their political identity. In doing so, he taught subsequent generations the true principles of self-government. These can still help Americans find common ground for promoting a common future as both a free and united people.

Notes

1. Abraham Lincoln, "Speech at a Republican Banquet, Chicago, Illinois," December 10, 1856, in *The Collected Works of Abraham Lincoln*, ed. Roy P. Basler, vol. 2, *1848–1858* (Rutgers University Press, 1953), 385.

2. Abraham Lincoln, "Speech at Springfield, Illinois," July 17, 1858, in *The Collected Works of Abraham Lincoln*, 2:50. He observed,

> We had gone through our struggle and secured our own independence. The framers of the Constitution found the institution of slavery amongst their other institutions at the time. They found that by an effort to eradicate it, they might lose much of what they had already gained. They were obliged to bow to the necessity.

3. Abraham Lincoln, "Address at Cooper Institute, New York City," February 27, 1860, in *The Collected Works of Abraham Lincoln*, vol. 3, *1858–1860*, 535. Lincoln said of the Founding Fathers, "*As those fathers marked it, so let it be again marked, as an evil not to be extended, but to be tolerated and protected only because of and so far as its actual presence among us makes that toleration and protection a necessity.*"

4. Abraham Lincoln to George Robertson, August 15, 1855, in *The Collected Works of Abraham Lincoln*, 2:318. Lincoln lamented, "That spirit which desired the peaceful extinction of slavery, has itself become extinct, with the *occasion*, and the *men* of the Revolution."

5. Abraham Lincoln, "Speech at Chicago, Illinois," July 10, 1858, in *The Collected Works of Abraham Lincoln*, 2:501.

6. Lincoln, "Speech at Chicago, Illinois," 2:488–89, 499–500.

7. *The New York Times*, "Mr. Douglas in His Native State—His Speech at Burlington, Vt.," August 2, 1860, https://www.nytimes.com/1860/08/02/archives/mr-douglas-in-his-native-state-his-speech-at-burlington-vt.html.

8. Stephen A. Douglas, "First Debate with Stephen A. Douglas at Ottawa, Illinois," August 21, 1858, in *The Collected Works of Abraham Lincoln*, 3:8, 12.

9. Stephen A. Douglas, "Speech of Stephen A. Douglas: Chicago, July 9, 1858," in *The Lincoln–Douglas Debates of 1858*, ed. Robert W. Johannsen (Oxford University Press, 1965), 29.

10. Douglas, "Speech of Stephen A. Douglas," in Johannsen, *The Lincoln–Douglas Debates of 1858*, 30.

11. John C. Breckinridge, "Speech of Mr. Breckinridge at Frankfort," *The New York Times*, July 25, 1860, https://www.nytimes.com/1860/07/25/archives/politics-in-kentucky-speech-of-mr-breckinridge-at-frankfort-mr.html.

12. John C. Breckinridge, "Speech of Hon. John C. Breckinridge [. . .]" (Washington, DC, 1860), 6, https://archive.org/details/speechofhonjohncoobrec/page/n1/mode/2up.

13. University of California, Santa Barbara, American Presidency Project, "Democratic Party Platform (Breckinridge Faction) of 1860," https://www.presidency.ucsb.edu/documents/democratic-party-platform-breckinridge-faction-1860.

14. Breckinridge, "Speech of Hon. John C. Breckinridge [. . .]," 8.

15. Breckinridge, "Speech of Hon. John C. Breckinridge [. . .]," 15.

16. Confederate Const. of 1861, art. I, § 9, cl. 4.

17. J. H. Thornwell, *Our Danger and Our Duty* (Southern Guardian Steam-Power Press, 1862), 5, https://docsouth.unc.edu/imls/thornwell/thornwel.html.

18. Lincoln, "Address at Cooper Institute," 4:535, 550.

19. Abraham Lincoln, "Address Delivered at the Dedication of the Cemetery at Gettysburg," November 19, 1863, in *The Collected Works of Abraham Lincoln*, vol. 7, *1863–1864*, 23.

20. Lincoln, "Address Delivered at the Dedication of the Cemetery at Gettysburg."

21. Lincoln, "Address Delivered at the Dedication of the Cemetery at Gettysburg."

22. Abraham Lincoln, "Address to the New Jersey Senate at Trenton, New Jersey," February 21, 1861, in *The Collected Works of Abraham Lincoln*, vol. 4, *1860–1861*, 236.

23. Lincoln, "Address to the New Jersey Senate at Trenton, New Jersey."

24. Abraham Lincoln, "Speech at New Haven, Connecticut," March 6, 1860, in *The Collected Works of Abraham Lincoln*, 4:18.

25. Abraham Lincoln, "Speech at Hartford, Connecticut," March 5, 1860, in *The Collected Works of Abraham Lincoln*, 4:5.

26. Abraham Lincoln, "Speech at Peoria, Illinois," October 16, 1854, in *The Collected Works of Abraham Lincoln*, 2:255.

27. Lincoln, "Speech at Peoria, Illinois," 2:276.

28. Dred Scott v. Sandford, 60 US 393, 410 (1857).

29. Stephen A. Douglas, "Fifth Debate with Stephen A. Douglas, at Galesburg, Illinois," October 7, 1858, in *The Collected Works of Abraham Lincoln*, 3:216.

30. Stephen A. Douglas, "Speech Delivered at Springfield, Ill. by Senator S. A. Douglas," July 17, 1858, Northern Illinois University Digital Library, https://digital.lib.niu.edu/islandora/object/niu-lincoln%3A35822.

31. Douglas, "Speech at Springfield, Illinois."

32. Ill. Const. of 1848, art. VI, § 1; and Ill. Const. of 1848, art. VIII, § 1.

33. Rodney O. Davis and Douglas L. Wilson, ed., *The Lincoln–Douglas Debates* (University of Illinois Press, 2008), 325–26.

34. Office of the Illinois Secretary of State, "Illinois Black Law (1853)," 100 Most Valuable Documents at the Illinois State Archives, https://www.ilsos.gov/departments/archives/online_exhibits/100_documents/1853-black-law.html.

35. Douglas, "First Debate with Stephen A. Douglas at Ottawa, Illinois," 3:4; Stephen A. Douglas, "Second Debate with Stephen A. Douglas at Freeport, Illinois," August 27, 1858, in *The Collected Works of Abraham Lincoln*, 3:56; Stephen A. Douglas, "Third Debate with Stephen A. Douglas at Jonesboro, Illinois," September 15, 1858, in *The Collected Works of Abraham Lincoln*, 3:106; Stephen A. Douglas, "Fourth Debate with Stephen A. Douglas at Charleston, Illinois," September 18, 1858, in *The Collected Works of Abraham Lincoln*, 3:176; Douglas, "Fifth Debate with Stephen A. Douglas, at Galesburg, Illinois," 3:215; Stephen A. Douglas, "Sixth Debate with Stephen A. Douglas,

at Quincy, Illinois," October 13, 1858, in *The Collected Works of Abraham Lincoln*, 3:261; and Stephen A. Douglas, "Seventh and Last Debate with Stephen A. Douglas at Alton, Illinois," October 15, 1858, in *The Collected Works of Abraham Lincoln*, 3:296.

36. Abraham Lincoln, "Speech at Springfield, Illinois," June 26, 1857, in *The Collected Works of Abraham Lincoln*, 2:406.

37. US Const. pmbl.

38. Lincoln, "Speech at Springfield, Illinois," June 26, 1857, 2:405.

39. See Alexander Keyssar, *The Right to Vote: The Contested History of Democracy in the United States*, rev. ed. (Basic Books, 2009).

40. Lincoln, "Speech at Springfield, Illinois," June 26, 1857, 2:406.

41. Abraham Lincoln, "'A House Divided': Speech at Springfield, Illinois," June 16, 1858, in *The Collected Works of Abraham Lincoln*, 2:467.

42. Douglas, "Fifth Debate with Stephen A. Douglas, at Galesburg, Illinois," 3:216.

43. Robert W. Johannsen, *Stephen A. Douglas* (Oxford University Press, 1973), 816–17; and S. 52, 36th Cong. art. 14, § 1 (1860).

44. "Nor shall any state deprive any person of life, liberty, or property, without due process of law; nor deny to any person within its jurisdiction the equal protection of the laws." US Const. amend. XIV, § 1.

45. Abraham Lincoln to Henry L. Pierce and Others, April 6, 1859, in *The Collected Works of Abraham Lincoln*, 3:375.

46. Lincoln to Pierce and Others, 3:375–76.

47. Lincoln to Pierce and Others, 3:376. Compare Thomas Jefferson, "Manners," query 18 in *Notes on the State of Virginia*, in *The Portable Thomas Jefferson*, ed. Merrill D. Peterson (Penguin Books, 1975), 215.

> And can the liberties of a nation be thought secure when we have removed their only firm basis, a conviction in the minds of the people that these liberties are the gift of God? That they are not to be violated but with his wrath? Indeed I tremble for my country when I reflect that God is just: that his justice cannot sleep forever.

48. Lincoln to Pierce and Others.

49. Alexander H. Stephens, quoted in Abraham Lincoln to Alexander H. Stephens, December 22, 1860, in *The Collected Works of Abraham Lincoln*, 4:161n1.

50. Abraham Lincoln, "Fragment on the Constitution and the Union," ca. January 1861, in *The Collected Works of Abraham Lincoln*, 4:168.

51. Lincoln, "Fragment on the Constitution and the Union," 4:169.

52. Confederate Const., art. I, § 9, cl. 4. As president, Lincoln never conceded a right of any American state to separate from the federal union under a constitutional or legal principle of "secession," calling it a "sophism" and "rebellion thus sugar-coated." See Abraham Lincoln, "Message to Congress in Special Session," July 4, 1861, in *The Collected Works of Abraham Lincoln*, 4:433. In his most pointed criticism of the alleged right to secession, Lincoln described it as "the essence of anarchy" at his first inauguration

as president. See Abraham Lincoln, "First Inaugural Address—Final Text," March 4, 1861, in *The Collected Works of Abraham Lincoln*, 4:268.

53. Alexander H. Stephens, "Cornerstone Speech," speech, Savannah, GA, March 21, 1861, American Battlefield Trust, https://www.battlefields.org/learn/primary-sources/cornerstone-speech.

54. Stephens, "Cornerstone Speech."

55. Stephens, "Cornerstone Speech."

56. Lincoln, "Speech at Peoria, Illinois," 2:266.

57. Abraham Lincoln to Albert G. Hodges, April 4, 1864, in *The Collected Works of Abraham Lincoln*, 7:281.

58. Abraham Lincoln to Horace Greeley, in *The Collected Works of Abraham Lincoln*, vol. 5, *1861–1862*, 388–89.

59. Abraham Lincoln, "Emancipation Proclamation," January 1, 1863, in *The Collected Works of Abraham Lincoln*, vol. 6, *1862–63*, 29.

60. Lincoln, "Emancipation Proclamation."

61. Frederick Douglass to Samuel J. May, January 28, 1863, in *Measuring the Man: The Writings of Frederick Douglass on Abraham Lincoln*, ed. Lucas E. Morel and Jonathan W. White (Reedy Press, 2025), 82.

62. Lincoln, "Emancipation Proclamation," 6:30.

63. Lincoln to Pierce and Others, 3:376.

64. Lincoln, "Speech at Hartford, Connecticut," 4:3.

4

The Founding of Frederick Douglass

JUSTIN DRIVER

On July 5, 1852, in Rochester, New York, as Frederick Douglass strode to the lectern at the august Corinthian Hall to deliver an Independence Day speech before a packed audience of almost six hundred people, he fought a significant bout of anxiety.

Douglass was not, of course, a man who grew nervous lightly. Even at the tender age of 34, the former slave had already become a prominent abolitionist, an acclaimed author, and a revered orator. Indeed, Douglass rose to fame in no small part due to his ability to exhibit uncommon mettle. As a young man, Douglass not only withstood ritualized beatings at the hands of an infamous "slave breaker," but he also dared to emancipate himself by escaping slavery. Since his entrance into public life, moreover, supporters of the existing racial order sometimes found Douglass's unyielding abolitionist message so vile that they opted to assault the messenger. In 1843, for example, Douglass's remarks promoting racial equality in Pendleton, Indiana, enraged a white mob, who beat him so severely that he suffered a loss of consciousness and a broken right hand.

Such prior brushes with danger, however, did nothing to prevent Douglass from experiencing the jitters in Rochester on that July afternoon as he listened to the Reverend Robert Raymond perform an introductory reading of the Declaration of Independence and prepared to deliver his address. Following the Declaration's recitation, observers noted that Douglass's hands trembled as he gripped his prepared remarks, which he opened by confessing to the assembled masses that he was experiencing "a quailing sensation."[1]

Douglass need not have been worried. When he concluded the speech now known as "What to the Slave Is the Fourth of July?," the audience responded rapturously, leaping to their feet to confer what one person called "a universal burst of applause."[2] Today, even as Douglass's speech begins inching toward its bicentennial, that initial ovation has not yet fully subsided. If anything, the applause has only grown louder.

"What to the Slave Is the Fourth of July?" long ago became required reading in high school and college curricula throughout the nation.[3] Distinguished scholars have, moreover, bathed Douglass's address in a sea of superlatives. Harvard Law School's Randall Kennedy has called it "the most damning critique of American hypocrisy ever uttered."[4] Historian William McFeely labeled it "perhaps the greatest antislavery oration ever given."[5] In David Blight's monumental biography of Douglass, he similarly deemed the address "nothing less than the rhetorical masterpiece of American abolitionism."[6] Going further, Blight called it "one of the greatest speeches of American history," one that "transcended his audience as well as Corinthian Hall" to enter the "realm inhabited by great art that would last long after he and this history were gone."[7]

It is not difficult to understand why Douglass's address has won such fervent admiration. The speech is rhetorically and emotionally powerful, advancing pungent criticism of how the United States has too often failed to honor its lofty ideals. It is hard to imagine a more eloquent spokesman for this proposition than the mighty Douglass. He not only knew the peculiar institution's base inequality intimately but communicated more effectively than anyone else the horrors of how slavery continued to cast a pall over antebellum America.

Today's veneration of Douglass's speech is surely attributable to widespread esteem for the speaker himself. Although Douglass was a divisive figure in his own time, he has now, improbably, achieved universal acclaim in the 21st century—an age defined by notorious, deep-seated polarization. The political left has, of course, long championed Douglass, and Democratic elected officials—including President Barack Obama—continue to hail him.[8]

Perhaps more surprisingly, the modern Republican Party has also begun extolling Douglass. In a 2013 ceremony at the US Capitol honoring the installation of a new bronze statue of Douglass, members of the GOP's congressional delegation donned large buttons proclaiming "Frederick Douglass Was a Republican."[9] In February 2017, not long after entering the Oval Office, President Donald Trump affirmed Douglass's place in the American pantheon during a Black History Month speech:

> I am very proud now that we have a museum on the National Mall where people can learn about Reverend King, so many other things, Frederick Douglass is an example of somebody who's done an amazing job and is getting recognized more and more, I notice.[10]

Remarking in 2021 upon Douglass's ubiquitous political appeal, Kennedy astutely observed: "Now *everyone* wants a piece of Frederick Douglass."[11] (Emphasis added.)

This same phenomenon appears in the judicial sphere, as jurists of quite distinct stripes all assert that Douglass would have supported their positions. Most prominently, Justice Clarence Thomas cited and quoted Douglass in *Zelman v. Simmons-Harris*, *Grutter v. Bollinger*, and *McDonald v. City of Chicago*, three blockbuster decisions respectively centered on school vouchers, affirmative action, and gun rights.[12]

But more recently, the Supreme Court's liberals have also ushered Douglass to center stage. Perhaps in response to Thomas's conspicuous invocation in *Grutter*, in which he argued that Douglass would have detested affirmative action, Justice Ketanji Brown Jackson's and Justice Sonia Sotomayor's dissenting opinions in *Students for Fair Admissions v. Harvard* both invoked Douglass.[13] The person black Americans once routinely referred to as "the Great Frederick," Jackson and Sotomayor asserted, should actually be understood to support affirmative action.[14] There is perhaps no better testament to Douglass's central position in American intellectual culture than the fact that jurisprudentially and ideologically opposed

Supreme Court justices now feel compelled to wield dueling quotations regarding how that eminence would have viewed modern admissions policies in elite higher education.

Given Douglass's widespread appeal today, it is with considerable trepidation—indeed, a quailing sensation—that I now venture criticism of Douglass's "What to the Slave Is the Fourth of July?" oration. To avoid causing misunderstanding, let me be clear at the outset that I, too, worship at the altar of Saint Frederick. His astonishing life—which traversed the path from slavery to not just freedom but the very apex of American intellectual life—deserves the honored place it has attained. His writing and thinking profoundly improved our nation and the world.

Douglass's example also vitally improved my life. I grew up in Washington, DC, east of the Anacostia River, within shouting distance of the Great Frederick's estate. That home became the Frederick Douglass National Historic Site in 1988, when I was 12 years old. I was keenly aware at an early age that just down the road from my house, not even one century earlier, a person who began life enslaved (and therefore would have been expected to die illiterate) somehow managed to rise and become one of the signature figures of American letters.

When I first read the revealingly titled *Narrative of the Life of Frederick Douglass, an American Slave: Written by Himself*, the book captured my full attention, at once haunting and mesmerizing me in a way that no other book had. Douglass is thus one of my childhood heroes, one whom I have not outgrown in these past four decades, nor do I anticipate ever doing so. I hold him in such regard that even these days when I teach his writing to my constitutional law students at Yale, I sometimes make a point of referring to the work of *Justice* Douglass—an honorific I bestow on no other figure who did not actually occupy a seat on the Supreme Court. I therefore heartily endorse the view of Harvard Law School's Annette Gordon-Reed, who has argued that "by any measure, Douglass should be considered a Founder of the country."[15]

Nevertheless, no person—not even Douglass—stands above criticism. Some esteemed theorists have, understandably, invoked Douglass for the proposition that the Fourth of July and black people go together like oil and water. For example, the philosopher Charles W. Mills has written that "Douglass saw, correctly, that July Fourth belonged to white Americans rather than to all Americans, and his anger at this appropriation continues to resound with us."[16] But as I argue in this chapter, such racialized understandings of who can legitimately lay claim to the Fourth of July are unduly constrained. The Fourth of July gave birth to the Declaration of Independence, and that document sparked more than the American Revolution against Britain. The Declaration's high-minded language has inspired many other revolts against oppression—including against white supremacy in the United States.

Douglass's famous Rochester oration thus would have been considerably improved had he lavished much greater attention on the Declaration's liberatory text and its larger meaning. That approach would have enabled him to emphasize the Declaration's resonant commitments to liberty and equality. Even if its signatories did not initially understand those commitments to include black Americans, abolitionists and proponents of racial equality nonetheless might extol the Declaration as inexorably, if inadvertently, paving the path toward racial liberation. On this account, the Fourth of July merited celebration—even in the grimmest days of slavery—because its soaring text ultimately facilitated the demise of that American atrocity. Black Americans have throughout American history rallied around the Declaration in their ongoing, never-ending efforts to perfect the American egalitarian project.

As we mark the document's semiquincentennial, it is essential to recall how the Declaration has often inspired courageous black Americans fighting for racial equality. In recovering several notable instances when black people have laid claim to the Declaration's emancipatory text, I hope to not only honor their efforts but insist further that the Fourth of July is mine—and ours.

A Document for White People?

Although the Declaration of Independence was recited in Corinthian Hall immediately before Douglass began his address, his remarks almost completely disregarded the Declaration's text. Instead, Douglass almost exclusively lambasted the nation's failure to ensure black people received the blessings of liberty. At the speech's outset, Douglass repeatedly and pointedly used the second person to address his overwhelmingly white audience about the Fourth of July's meaning.[17] "It is the birthday of *your* National Independence, and of *your* political freedom," Douglass contended.[18] "The freedom gained is *yours*; and *you*, therefore, may properly celebrate this anniversary. The 4th of July is the first great fact in *your* nation's history."[19] (Emphasis added.)

Douglass asserted that black people—particularly the enslaved—had scant occasion for celebrating the Declaration. Inviting a black person to commemorate the Fourth of July, Douglass insisted, amounted to sheer ridicule:

> Why am I called upon to speak here to-day? What have I, or those I represent, to do with your national independence? Are the great principles of political freedom and of natural justice, embodied in that Declaration of Independence, extended to us?[20]

Douglass made it clear that he believed Independence Day was a holiday exclusively for white people. "This Fourth of July is *yours*, not *mine*," he stated. "*You* may rejoice, *I* must mourn."[21] (Emphasis in original.) Douglass noted that, for the enslaved, Independence Day served as a source not of inspiration but rather of despair. Channeling "the slave's point of view," Douglass added: "Fellow-citizens, above your national, tumultuous joy, I hear the mournful wail of millions! whose chains, heavy and grievous yesterday, are, to-day, rendered more intolerable by the jubilee shouts that reach them."[22]

These remarks set the stage for Douglass's core claim, which provides the speech's modern handle and has now achieved a celebrated status:

> What, to the American slave, is your 4th of July? I answer; a day that reveals to him, more than all other days in the year, the gross injustice and cruelty to which he is the constant victim. To him, your celebration is a sham; your boasted liberty, an unholy license; your national greatness, swelling vanity; your sounds of rejoicing are empty and heartless; your denunciation of tyrants, brass fronted impudence; your shouts of liberty and equality, hollow mockery; your prayers and hymns, your sermons and thanksgivings, with all your religious parade and solemnity, are, to Him, mere bombast, fraud, deception, impiety, and hypocrisy—a thin veil to cover up crimes which would disgrace a nation of savages. There is not a nation on the earth guilty of practices more shocking and bloody than are the people of the United States, at this very hour.[23]

This searing denunciation of the United States informs a significant tradition in black political thought.[24] Reading these words today, it is striking how Douglass's remarks anticipate acerbic criticisms leveled by Marcus Garvey, Malcolm X, and—more recently—Rev. Jeremiah Wright, in his sermon that proclaimed not "God Bless America" but instead "God damn America."[25]

The foregoing excerpts are among the most familiar quotations from Douglass's speech. In recent years, a small number of observers—often in conservative outlets—have suggested that such excerpts provide a misleading, unduly jaundiced impression of Douglass's speech. These revisionists seize upon some of Douglass's statements to suggest that he held the nation's founding and founders in a far more flattering light than is generally understood. Revisionists further lament that Douglass's speech is typically excerpted, and the more overtly patriotic sentiments invariably end up on the cutting room floor.[26]

But these protestations should not carry the day. Apart from Abraham Lincoln's famously concise Gettysburg Address, virtually all well-known American speeches are reprinted in partial form rather than in their entirety. In the world of canonical oration, synecdoche is the rule rather than the exception. The common excerpts of Douglass's address, moreover, do not significantly distort his central message.

Instead, the revisionists alight upon what are in fact stray remarks provided in the course of a very long address to contend that Douglass advanced views of the United States that are more compatible with the revisionists' own. But in this instance, at least, the standard view of Douglass's address accurately conveys his dominant thrust. Legal scholars Jack Balkin and Sanford Levinson, who have played a key role in canonizing Douglass's work in constitutional circles, have accurately summed up the matter as follows: "One of Douglass's most famous speeches—on the Fourth of July—emphasized that the Declaration of Independence was only a declaration for white people."[27]

It is entirely commendable, of course, that Douglass faulted the United States for refusing to see how chattel slavery could not be tolerated in a society predicated on egalitarianism. In the 1850s, the persistent contradiction between America's original sin and its highest ideals deserved to be identified and rejected on every possible occasion. But it is also more than plausible to read the Declaration of Independence as paving the road to racial equality and the abolition of slavery. Even if Thomas Jefferson failed to carry the implication of his liberatory cry to its natural, emancipationist conclusion, supporters of racial equality could view—and, indeed, often have viewed—the Declaration as a tool of racial liberation.

On this account, when Douglass asked rhetorically in Corinthian Hall, "What have I, or those I represent, to do with your national independence?" a powerful response would have been: *"Everything."* Such a response would have proceeded to pay careful attention to the Declaration's text. Indeed, eight years after he spoke in Rochester, Douglass himself creatively and masterfully demonstrated how black Americans could

construe a different foundational American text—the US Constitution—
as a document that promotes racial equality and slavery's abolition.

An Instrument of Liberation

In 1860, Douglass delivered a brilliant speech in Glasgow, Scotland, titled
"The Constitution of the United States: Is It Pro-Slavery or Anti-Slavery?"[28]
The Constitution at that time, of course, did not yet include the 13th, 14th,
or 15th Amendments—known collectively as the Reconstruction Amendments. Therefore, the most straightforward reading of the pre–Civil War
Constitution may well have deemed the document inexorably proslavery.
In 1847, a young Douglass had condemned the Constitution in no uncertain terms, advancing the constitutional vision of doom associated with
William Lloyd Garrison. "I have not, I cannot have, any love for this country, as such, or for its Constitution," Douglass said then. "I desire to see
its overthrow as speedily as possible, and its Constitution shivered in a
thousand fragments."[29]

Over time, however, Douglass changed his mind and firmly rejected
Garrisonian anti-constitutionalism. In Glasgow, he boldly asserted that
the Constitution, properly understood, should be viewed as resolutely
antislavery. How did Douglass defend that arresting claim? His critical
move elevated the Constitution's text to paramount importance and
simultaneously made clear that any intentions the framers may have pri-
vately entertained but did not reduce to text were wholly irrelevant:

> The intentions of those who framed the Constitution . . . are to
> be respected so far, and so far only, as we find those intentions
> plainly stated in the Constitution. It would . . . lead to endless
> confusion and mischiefs, if, instead of looking to the written
> paper itself, for its meaning, it were attempted to make us
> search it out, in the secret motives . . . of some of the men who
> took part in writing it. It was what they said that was adopted

by the people, not what they were ashamed or afraid to say, and really omitted to say.[30]

Today, of course, "textualism" and "originalism" are often used synonymously. But here Douglass can be viewed as pulling apart those two approaches, distinguishing textualism from original-intent originalism.[31] When text and original intent collide, Douglass argued, the Constitution's text must prevail.

Emphasizing constitutional text enabled Douglass to capitalize upon the fact that the Constitution's framers declined to use the word "slavery" or "slaves" throughout the entire document. That diffidence provided an opening, which Douglass proceeded to waltz right through. Douglass noted that the Constitution opens with the majestic words "We the People" and draws no distinctions among the people, racial or otherwise:

> Its language is 'we the people;' not we the white people, not even we the citizens, not we the privileged class, not we the high, not we the low, but we the people; . . . and, if Negroes are people, they are included in the benefits for which the Constitution of America was ordained and established.[32]

Those who believed that the Constitution protects slavery, Douglass contended, do so by smuggling in their own predilections that were not included in the instrument itself. "The American Constitution is pressed into the service of slavery," he stated, "by assuming that the Constitution does not mean what it says, and that it says what it does not mean; by disregarding the written Constitution, and interpreting it in the light of a secret understanding."[33] Rather than leading with constitutional text, Douglass wrote, wrongheaded interpreters of the document prioritized extratextual sources: "They go everywhere else for proof that the Constitution is pro-slavery but to the Constitution itself."[34]

With the textual foundation established, Douglass then advanced numerous arguments that particular constitutional provisions should actually be viewed as militating against slavery. Consider here two of Douglass's ingenious arguments, which transform putatively proslavery constitutional text into antislavery provisions. First, Douglass focused on what is today known as the three-fifths compromise in Article I, Section 2, clause 3, which determined that a state's number of congressional representatives would be derived from its total population, including "three fifths of all other Persons" (i.e., slaves).[35] While this provision might be thought to countenance slavery, Douglass insisted that it actually undermined the peculiar institution.

> [The clause] is a downright disability laid upon the slaveholding States; one which deprives those States of two-fifths of their natural basis of representation. A black man in a free State is worth just two-fifths more than a black man in a slave State, as a basis of political power under the Constitution. Therefore, instead of encouraging slavery, the Constitution encourages freedom by giving an increase of 'two-fifths' of political power to free over slave States.[36]

Second, Douglass turned his attention to Article I, Section 8, clause 15, which empowered Congress to form militias "to . . . suppress Insurrections."[37] Although this constitutional provision was routinely called "the 'slave insurrection' clause," Douglass hastened to add that "in truth, there is no such clause."[38] But even if there were such a constitutional clause, he argued, its existence would nevertheless point in an antislavery direction. Douglass argued:

> If it should turn out that slavery is a source of insurrection, that there is no security from insurrection while slavery lasts, why, the Constitution would be best obeyed by putting an end to slavery, and an anti-slavery Congress would do that very thing.[39]

Well before the passage of the Reconstruction Amendments, Douglass thus vividly contended in Glasgow that the Constitution should be viewed as an instrument of liberation. In so doing, he provided an early, inspiring example of how even the most scorned, marginalized people in American history could nevertheless view one of the nation's foundational texts as advancing their egalitarian mission. Even if Douglass's constitutional readings would not win prizes for historical plausibility, the very fact that a formerly enslaved person eloquently cast his lot with the Constitution helped make a vision that could have been dismissed as a mere provocation into reality. If Douglass's transgressive textual readings could effectively embrace the Constitution as an antislavery document, that approach surely could have also reaped fruit with the Declaration of Independence.

Douglass's Declaration—and Ours

Employing the textual techniques that Douglass displayed in Glasgow regarding the Constitution reveals, not surprisingly, that the Declaration of Independence can readily be interpreted as an antislavery document. In my view, Douglass's Rochester address would have been significantly improved if he had expended greater intellectual energy parsing the Declaration's liberatory text. That opportunity was teed up nicely by Reverend Raymond's delivery of the Declaration immediately before Douglass spoke, but Douglass, alas, declined to avail himself of that compelling approach. Allow me here to pay homage to Douglass's constitutional textualism by briefly sketching how that methodology could have enabled him explicitly to claim the Declaration for himself— and his people.

Douglass could have, of course, started at the beginning. In 13 of the most famous words ever strung together, the Declaration asserted: "We hold these truths to be self-evident, that all men are created equal." In the spirit of Douglass's racially inclusive reading of the Constitution's preamble, one can easily imagine him insisting that the Declaration's most resonant language also did not draw racial lines.

The Declaration did not instruct that "all *white* men are created equal" but instead embraced a vision of egalitarianism that did not acknowledge racial boundaries. It did not say, moreover, that only "citizens" were created equal. Instead, the Declaration's notion of equality applied to all mankind, slaves included. Even if this notion were not "self-evident," as the Declaration itself insisted, recall that the Constitution—including in the three-fifths clause—repeatedly refers to the enslaved as "persons."[40] If that is not an acknowledgment of black humanity, then what is?

Textual support for the Declaration's antislavery reading would continue by considering the language that held among the God-given inalienable rights that mankind possesses "Life, Liberty and the pursuit of Happiness." But, of course, bondage quite literally prohibits slaves from realizing either their liberty or the ability to pursue happiness. Slavery's heavy chains render it impossible for those in its confines to move about the nation freely in the pursuit of joy, flourishing, or anything else, for that matter. To the contrary, one of slavery's foremost atrocities was the institution's blatant disregard for familial liberty and happiness, as it routinely licensed children being separated from their mothers and fathers at their enslavers' whims.

A text-driven understanding of the Declaration as an abolitionist document would emphasize that its dominant through lines sound in anti-despotic and anti-tyrannical motivations. While the Declaration casts King George III in the role of despot and tyrant, the larger principles that it embraces can also be viewed as rebuking the mini-despots and the mini-tyrants who ruled American plantations. The Declaration employs antiauthoritarian rhetoric in at least two critical instances. First, it states that "when a long train of abuses and usurpations . . . evinces a design to reduce [the people] under absolute despotism, it is their right, it is their duty, to throw off such Government, and to provide new Guards for their future security." One can easily imagine Douglass saying that the American slave knew more than a little something about the sorts of "abuses and usurpations" that yield "absolute despotism" and that adhering to the Declaration therefore demanded revolting against the slavocracy under which they toiled.

Second, as the Declaration shifts from abstract principles to concrete details, it notes: "The history of the present King of Great Britain is a history of repeated injuries and usurpations, all having in direct object the establishment of an absolute Tyranny." Douglass might argue that at least as much as the Declaration's signatories, the enslaved—including himself—knew very well that slavery's brutality and barbarity visited countless "injuries" and subjected those held in its clutches to "absolute Tyranny." While the signatories may have intended primarily to throw off the yoke of King George III's tyranny, Douglass might have argued that we should nonetheless honor their broader, stated ambitions to oppose the tyrant and the despot, in his many guises, who ruled on American soil.

Several items on the Declaration's bill of grievances against King George III also might be understood to apply with significant force against slaveholders. Consider three of those grievances and their underlying principles. The Declaration laments that King George III "has excited domestic insurrections amongst us." But as Douglass argued regarding the Constitution's "'slave insurrection' clause," the fact that many understood slavery's potential for fomenting domestic unrest suggests that the Declaration's anti-insurrection principle was in effect an antislavery provision.

In addition, the Declaration censured King George III for "plunder[ing] our seas, ravag[ing] our Coasts, burn[ing] our towns, and destroy[ing] the lives of our people." Although this grievance was aimed at Lord Dunmore's egregious behavior as royal governor of Virginia, Douglass could have seized upon it to argue not only against the transatlantic slave trade's rapacious treatment of innumerable African communities but also against the way slavery destroyed untold lives of people of African descent in America.

Finally, and most adventurously, Douglass could have noted that the Declaration condemned King George III "for Quartering large bodies of armed troops among us." Here, Jefferson was directing his particular ire at Parliament's 1765 Quartering Act, which entitled British soldiers to shelter in the American colonies. This grievance, of course, inspired the Constitution's Third Amendment, which provides that "no Soldier shall, in time of peace be quartered in any house, without the consent of the Owner, nor in time of war, but in a manner to be prescribed by law."[41] Given that the Supreme Court has recognized a right to privacy in no small part derived from the Third Amendment's prohibition on quartering soldiers, it would be possible to argue that the Declaration also recognized a proto-right to privacy.[42] And because the slaves' right to privacy was notable exclusively for its absence—in their inability to control who entered their most intimate quarters—the Declaration should along this dimension also be viewed as assuming an abolitionist character.

But even had Douglass laid extensive claim to the Declaration's liberatory promise in Corinthian Hall long ago, that would hardly have been a novel development in black American political thought. Instead, black people extolling the Declaration of Independence and its ideals is, with apologies to H. Rap Brown, as American as cherry pie.[43]

The Emancipatory Declaration

Celebrated black Americans have long laid claim to the Declaration of Independence, citing it as a vital source of inspiration in the struggles for racial equality and beyond. For example, in 1944, Howard University historian Rayford Logan published a remarkable collection of essays written by the era's preeminent black leaders and intellectuals in a volume titled simply *What the Negro Wants*. Mary McLeod Bethune, founder of the National Council of Negro Women, opened her contribution, on "Certain Unalienable Rights," with an extended analogy connecting the grievances motivating the Boston Tea Party in 1773 to the discontent swirling throughout urban black America in the 1940s.

Tyranny, Bethune insisted, arrives in different forms—including in the violence that white police officers too often visited upon black Americans. The urban unrest gripping Detroit and Los Angeles in the 1940s should be viewed as efforts to "achieve the ideals 'that all men are created equal, that they are endowed by their Creator with certain unalienable Rights, that among these are Life, Liberty, and the pursuit of Happiness,'" Bethune contended.[44] "Just as the Colonists at the Boston Tea Party wanted 'out' from under tyranny and oppression and taxation without representation . . . colored Americans want 'out.'"[45]

Bethune suggested that in the same manner as they looked to the American Revolution in their pursuit of racial equality on the domestic front, black Americans looked to the American Revolution as driving their fight against tyranny during World War II on the international front. She argued:

> All true Americans should not be surprised by this logical climax of American education. For several generations colored Americans have been brought up on the Boston Tea Party and the Declaration of Independence; on the principle of equality of opportunity, the possession of inalienable rights, the integrity and sanctity of the human personality. Along with other good Americans the Negro has been prepared to take his part in the fight against an enemy that threatens all these basic American principles.[46]

Bethune contended, in essence, that though black people wanted *out* of racial oppression, they also wanted *in* on the fight against fascism.

As editor of *The Crisis*, the NAACP's official organ, Roy Wilkins struck similar themes in his contribution to *What the Negro Wants*. "The Negro is here," Wilkins wrote. "He is thoroughly American. He thinks and lives in the American tradition. He learns from American text books about the Revolutionary war, about independence, the spirit of America—and equality."[47]

Wilkins's invocation of the American Revolution was hardly an isolated incident. In 1955, just after he ascended to become the NAACP's executive secretary, Wilkins suggested that ardent segregationists were destined to fail just as other seemingly implacable foes had failed throughout history—including during the 1770s. Defenders of Jim Crow, Wilkins argued, "say 'never' like the Romans before the coming of Christ; like King John before Magna Charta . . . like George III of England before the Declaration of Independence."[48]

In perhaps the Declaration's most celebrated invocation during the past century, Rev. Martin Luther King Jr. dedicated a key passage of the "I Have a Dream" speech in 1963 to contending that the civil rights movement carried on the American Revolution's central promise. In his inimitable tones, King asserted:

> When the architects of our republic wrote the magnificent words of the Constitution and the Declaration of Independence, they were signing a promissory note to which every American was to fall heir. This note was a promise that all men, yes, black men as well as white men, would be guaranteed the "unalienable Rights of Life, Liberty, and the pursuit of Happiness." . . .
>
> . . . So even though we face the difficulties of today and tomorrow, I still have a dream. It is a dream deeply rooted in the American dream.
>
> I have a dream that one day this nation will rise up and live out the true meaning of its creed: "We hold these truths to be self-evident, that all men are created equal."[49]

During the classical phase of the civil rights movement, King was far from alone in portraying its mission not as a castigation of American ideals but instead as a consecration of those ideals.

President Barack Obama, an attentive student of the civil rights movement, has repeatedly invoked the Declaration as a source of inspiration. For instance, toward the conclusion of his memoir *Dreams from My Father*, Obama acknowledged that legal study can sometimes seem abstract, mundane, and technocratic. "But that's not all the law is," he continued.[50] Obama then proceeded to connect the Declaration not only to Douglass but also to the modern march toward racial equality. "The law is also memory; the law also records a long-running conversation, a nation arguing with its conscience," he wrote. "*We hold these truths to be self-evident.* In those words, I hear the spirit of Douglass and Delany, as well as Jefferson and Lincoln; the struggles of Martin and Malcolm and unheralded marchers to bring these words to life."[51] (Emphasis in original.)

In his political debut on the national stage at the Democratic Party's convention in 2004, moreover, Obama memorably tied his own meteoric rise to the fulfillment of America's founding ideals. "I stand here knowing that my story is part of the larger American story, that I owe a debt to all of those who came before me, and that in no other country on Earth is my story even possible," he said.[52] American pride, Obama continued, derived not from our military might nor even our economic power:

> Our pride is based on a very simple premise, summed up in a declaration made over two hundred years ago: "We hold these truths to be self-evident, that all men are created equal, that they are endowed by their Creator with certain inalienable rights."[53]

When he delivered those words in 2004, Obama had recently secured Illinois's Democratic nomination for the US Senate. But those inspiring, patriotic remarks played a major role in propelling him into the White House only four years later.

It may be tempting to believe that black people claiming the Declaration as a liberatory text became possible only in the mid-20th century. On this account, criticizing Douglass for failing to make full use of the Declaration's textual promise in the 1850s—well before the abolition of slavery—would hold him to an impossible, ahistorical standard. Such objections, however, miss the mark.

Some black people claimed the Declaration as an emancipatory document as early as 1777—less than six months after John Hancock affixed his signature to the document. As Harvard University's Danielle Allen has highlighted, a free black man in Massachusetts named Prince Hall became "the first American to publicly use the language of the Declaration of Independence for a political purpose other than justifying war against Britain."[54] In a document filed with the Massachusetts legislature, Hall—joined by several fellow free black men—contended that the Declaration's language required abolishing race-based slavery in America.[55] Hall's call for slavery's abolition included repeated echoes of the Declaration, echoes which are (per Allen) italicized in the following excerpt:

> The petition of A Great Number of Blackes detained in a State of Slavery in the Bowels of a free & christian Country Humbly shuwith that your Petitioners Apprehend that Thay have in Common with all other men a *Natural and Unaliable Right to that freedom which the Grat—Parent of the Unavese hath Bestowed equalley on all menkind* and which they have Never forfuted by Any Compact or Agreement whatever—but thay wher Unjustly Dragged by the hand of cruel Power from their Derest frinds and sum of them Even torn from the Embraces of their tender Parents—from A popolous Plasant And plentiful cuntry And in Violation of *Laws of Nature and off Nations* And in defiance of all the tender feelings of humanity Brough hear Either to Be sold Like Beast of Burthen & Like them Condemnd to Slavery for Life.[56]

Hall's liberatory reading of the Declaration can thus be understood as anticipating Reverend King's peroration by a little less than two centuries.

Even Douglass himself ultimately understood the value that could flow from firmly, explicitly embracing the Fourth of July, portraying himself and black people generally not as somehow outside of founding American principles but instead as their rightful claimants. In 1862, a decade after his Rochester address, he delivered another, quite distinct Fourth of July address in a New York hamlet called Himrod Corners. Whereas Douglass's Rochester address is known the world over, the Himrod Corners speech has been all but forgotten.

The relatively small imprint of this speech is regrettable because it not only marks a critical inflection point in Douglass's thought but also makes for a fascinating juxtaposition with the Rochester oration. As Blight has emphasized, in the Himrod Corners address, Douglass—for the first time—referred to America's founding generation with not only the distancing second-person "your fathers" but also the intimate, first-person "our fathers."[57] Seldom in the history of American literature has the subtraction of a single letter made a more profound difference.

Instead of excoriating white Americans for failing to honor fully the Declaration's promise of liberty, Douglass encouraged them to make that promise real. "The claims of our fathers upon our memory, admiration and gratitude, are founded in the fact that they wisely, and bravely, and successfully met the crisis of their day," he stated. "And if the men of this generation would deserve well of posterity they must like their fathers, discharge the duties and responsibilities of their age."[58]

The deep problems confronting the United States in the 1860s, Douglass urged, could be remedied by returning to the high ideals articulated by the original founding generation. In this sense, he contended that the Civil War should be regarded as but an extension of the Revolutionary War. Just as the original founding generation "drew the sword for free and independent Government, Republican in its form, Democratic in its spirit," Douglass observed,

> the war of to-day on the part of the loyal north, the east and the west, is waged for the same grand and all commanding objects. We are only continuing the tremendous struggle, which your fathers, and my fathers began eighty-six years ago.[59]

Now, 163 years after Douglass made his pivotal turn, theorists in certain quarters doubt the wisdom of embracing America's governmental and intellectual foundations. While Douglass's posture in 1852 may be deeply fashionable today, we should not lose sight of the fact that his approach in 1862 is for the ages. Indeed, if Douglass, Bethune, Wilkins, King, and Hall

all found inspiration in the Declaration of Independence as they waged their battles for racial justice, who are we now to abandon that honorable tradition?

Notes

1. Frederick Douglass, "The Meaning of July Fourth for the Negro," speech, Rochester, NY, July 5, 1852, in *Frederick Douglass: Selected Speeches and Writings*, ed. Philip S. Foner (Lawrence Hill Books, 1999), 188. These opening paragraphs are drawn from a wide array of sources. See David W. Blight, *Frederick Douglass: Prophet of Freedom* (Simon & Schuster, 2018), 59–67, 134, 229–36; William S. McFeely, *Frederick Douglass* (W. W. Norton & Company, 1991), 44–48, 108–12, 172–73; James A. Colaiaco, *Frederick Douglass and the Fourth of July* (Palgrave Macmillan, 2006), 1–2, 7–8, 12, 23–24, 119–21; Brent Staples, "Frederick the Great," *The New York Times Book Review*, November 11, 2018; and David Levering Lewis, "The Great Frederick," *The New York Times*, February 17, 1991, https://www.nytimes.com/1991/02/17/books/the-great-frederick.html.

2. Blight, *Frederick Douglass*, 236.

3. See Andrew S. Bibby, "What to the Slave Is the Fourth of July?," *The Wall Street Journal*, July 2, 2014, https://www.wsj.com/articles/andrew-bibby-what-to-the-slave-is-the-fourth-of-july-1404342530.

4. Randall Kennedy, *Say It Loud! On Race, Law, History, and Culture* (Pantheon, 2021), 233.

5. McFeely, *Frederick Douglass*, 173.

6. Blight, *Frederick Douglass*, 230.

7. Blight, *Frederick Douglass*, 236.

8. Kennedy, *Say It Loud!*, 234.

9. Kennedy, *Say It Loud!* See also David W. Blight, "How the Right Co-Opts Frederick Douglass," *The New York Times*, February 13, 2018, https://www.nytimes.com/2018/02/13/opinion/right-coopts-frederick-douglass.html.

10. David A. Graham, "Donald Trump's Narrative of the Life of Frederick Douglass," *The Atlantic*, February 1, 2017, https://www.theatlantic.com/politics/archive/2017/02/frederick-douglass-trump/515292/.

11. Kennedy, *Say It Loud!*

12. Zelman v. Simmons-Harris, 536 US 639, 676, 684 (2002); Grutter v. Bollinger, 539 US 306, 349–50, 378 (2003); and McDonald v. City of Chicago, 561 US 742, 849–50 (2010).

13. Students for Fair Admissions v. Harvard, 600 US 181, 320, 386, 393 (2023).

14. "Black people called him the Great Frederick." Lewis, "The Great Frederick."

15. Annette Gordon-Reed, "Comment on *Frederick Douglass and the Two Constitutions: Proslavery and Antislavery*," *California Law Review* 111 (December 2023): 1909, 1913,

https://www.californialawreview.org/print/comment-on-frederick-douglass-and-the-two-constitutions-proslavery-and-antislavery.

16. Charles W. Mills, *Blackness Visible: Essays on Philosophy and Race* (Cornell University Press, 1998), 200.

17. Blight's biography effectively emphasizes this point. Blight, *Frederick Douglass*, 232.

18. Douglass, "The Meaning of July Fourth for the Negro," 189.

19. Douglass, "The Meaning of July Fourth for the Negro," 191.

20. Douglass, "The Meaning of July Fourth for the Negro," 194.

21. Douglass, "The Meaning of July Fourth for the Negro."

22. Douglass, "The Meaning of July Fourth for the Negro," 194–95.

23. Douglass, "The Meaning of July Fourth for the Negro," 196–97.

24. Kennedy, *Say It Loud!*, 235–37.

25. See ABC News, "Obama's Pastor: God Damn America, U.S. to Blame for 9/11," March 13, 2008, https://abcnews.go.com/Blotter/DemocraticDebate/story?id=4443788.

26. For examples of the revisionist approach, see Diana Schaub, "Frederick Douglass: The Constitution Militant," *The Georgetown Journal of Law & Public Policy* 22, no. 1 (2024): 137, 140, https://www.law.georgetown.edu/public-policy-journal/wp-content/uploads/sites/23/2024/06/GT-GLPP240006.pdf; Bibby, "What to the Slave Is the Fourth of July?"; and Stephen Sachs, "Good and Evil in the American Founding: The 2023 Vaughan Lecture on America's Founding Principles," *Harvard Journal of Law and Public Policy* 48, no. 1 (2025): 283, https://papers.ssrn.com/sol3/papers.cfm?abstract_id=4843831.

27. Jack M. Balkin and Sanford Levinson, "Frederick Douglass as Constitutionalist," *Maryland Law Review* 83, no. 1 (2023): 260, 279, https://digitalcommons.law.umaryland.edu/cgi/viewcontent.cgi?article=3984&context=mlr. "We gladly affirm that Douglass's Glasgow Address deserves a place in the canons of constitutional pedagogy." J. M. Balkin and Sanford Levinson, "The Canons of Constitutional Law," *Harvard Law Review* 111, no. 4 (1998): 1019, https://openyls.law.yale.edu/bitstream/handle/20.500.13051/1931/The_Canons_of_Constitutional_Law.pdf. For excerpts and a discussion of Douglass's Glasgow speech, see Sanford Levinson et al., *Processes of Constitutional Decisionmaking: Cases and Materials*, 8th ed. (Aspen Publishing, 2022), 292–97.

28. Frederick Douglass, "The Constitution of the United States: Is It Pro-Slavery or Antislavery?," speech, Glasgow, Scotland, March 26, 1860, in Foner, ed., *Frederick Douglass*, 380–89.

29. Frederick Douglass, "The Right to Criticize American Institutions," speech, American Anti-Slavery Society, May 11, 1847, in Foner, ed., *Frederick Douglass*, 77–78.

30. Douglass, "The Constitution of the United States," 381.

31. Most originalists today, of course, march behind the banner not of "original intent" but instead of "original public meaning." Douglass's move here bears a strong similarity to the move that Justice Antonin Scalia made regarding originalism in the 1980s. For a note explaining that Scalia re-centered originalism's focus, moving the

search from "original intent" to "original meaning," see Justin Driver, "Divine Justice," *The New Republic*, September 29, 2014, 40–42.

32. Douglass, "The Constitution of the United States," 387.

33. Douglass, "The Constitution of the United States," 388.

34. Douglass, "The Constitution of the United States."

35. US Const. art. I, § 2, cl. 3.

36. Douglass, "The Constitution of the United States," 384.

37. US Const. art. I, § 8, cl. 15.

38. Douglass, "The Constitution of the United States," 384.

39. Douglass, "The Constitution of the United States," 385.

40. See US Const. art. I, § 2, cl. 3; and US Const. art. I, § 9, cl. 1.

41. US Const. amend. III.

42. For grounding the right to privacy in the Third Amendment, see Griswold v. Connecticut, 381 US 479, 484 (1965).

43. For quoting H. Rap Brown's statement that "violence is as American as cherry pie," see John Herbers, "Violence; It Is as American as Cherry Pie," *The New York Times*, June 8, 1969, https://www.nytimes.com/1969/06/08/archives/violence-it-is-as-american-as-cherry-pie.html. I will leave it to others to parse whether apple pie is the more prototypically American dessert.

44. Mary McLeod Bethune, "Certain Unalienable Rights," in Rayford Logan, ed., *What the Negro Wants* (University of North Carolina Press, 1944), 248, 249.

45. Bethune, "Certain Unalienable Rights," 249–50.

46. Bethune, "Certain Unalienable Rights," 250.

47. Roy Wilkins, "The Negro Wants Full Equality," in Logan, *What the Negro Wants*, 113, 130.

48. Roy Wilkins, "The Conspiracy to Deny Equality," in *The Voice of Black America: Major Speeches by Negroes in the United States 1797–1973*, ed. Philip S. Foner (Simon & Schuster, 1972).

49. Martin Luther King Jr., "I Have a Dream," speech, Washington, DC, August 28, 1963, in *A Call to Conscience: The Landmark Speeches of Dr. Martin Luther King, Jr.*, ed. Clayborne Carson and Kris Shepard (Grand Central Publishing, 2001), 81, 82, 85. (Audience responses cleaned up.)

50. Barack Obama, *Dreams from My Father: A Story of Race and Inheritance* (Times Books, 1995), 437.

51. Obama, *Dreams from My Father*, 437.

52. Barack Obama, "The Audacity of Hope," speech, 2004 Democratic National Convention, Boston, July 27, 2004, in *We Are the Change We Seek: The Speeches of Barack Obama*, ed. E. J. Dionne Jr. and Joy-Ann Reid (Bloomsbury, 2017), 5, 7.

53. Obama, "The Audacity of Hope," 7.

54. Danielle Allen, "A Forgotten Black Founding Father," *The Atlantic*, March 2021, 42, 44, https://www.theatlantic.com/magazine/archive/2021/03/prince-hall-forgotten-founder/617791/.

55. Allen, "A Forgotten Black Founding Father," 44.

56. Allen, "A Forgotten Black Founding Father."

57. Blight, *Frederick Douglass*, 368.

58. Douglass, "The Slaveholders' Rebellion," speech, Himrods Corners, Yates County, NY, July 4, 1862, in Foner, ed., *Frederick Douglass*, 495, 496.

59. Douglass, "The Slaveholders' Rebellion," 495, 496.

5

Frederick Douglass's Civic Education

DIANA SCHAUB

In his most famous speech, "What to the Slave Is the Fourth of July?," delivered 76 years after 1776, Frederick Douglass found hope in the thought that the nation was young. "Still in the impressible stage," the United States might be capable of moral maturation. The improvement Douglass desired—the abolition of slavery—did not require repudiating the nation's origins; "high lessons of wisdom, of justice and of truth," which could "give direction to her destiny," might be gleaned from the birthday of national independence. "Were the nation older," he said, "the patriot's heart might be sadder."[1]

Our nation is now considerably older. In this semiquincentennial year, must our hearts be sad? Perhaps there are grounds for hope in the fact that even old nations are continually refreshed by young citizens. Like the poor, the young will always be with us. But that means the task of education is always with us too. Birthright citizenship makes citizens only in a technical or formal sense; only a properly formative education can make us into the sorts of citizens our republic requires. Unfortunately, many students today are shaped largely by their early and sustained miseducation. They are not, in the deeper sense, students at all. They are not attentive to language, not open to evidence and argument, not curious about the past, not observant of the world around them. Behind these failures of intellect, there is a more profound disorder of the heart. Young Americans are not patriots; moreover, they regard patriotism with suspicion. This creates a dilemma for civic learning, since all learning begins in love. Budding entomologists just love bugs. That kind of pure and simple attachment is not possible in the political realm.

In my experience as a college teacher, most students arrive with serious reservations about the American founding. It turns out that those reservations are rooted in the American attachment to equality—students seem unaware that their very objection pays tribute to the founders' declaration of equality as the premise of the nation. Instead of understanding how the founders shaped the moral commitments of succeeding generations, students have been instructed that the founders were either hypocrites or worse than hypocrites. Either they included blacks in the human family, in which case they were hypocrites for not immediately ending slavery and establishing equality, or they didn't even consider blacks to be human, in which case they were racist fools. Either interpretation leads young people to dismiss the founding generation and feel shame rather than gratitude toward their inheritance. Since they regard themselves as already morally superior, maturation is not their aim.

Students will hold themselves aloof from civic learning until their moral qualms about the nation's origins are addressed. The separation of powers, checks and balances, and all the ingenious discoveries of the "new science of politics" lie flat on the page, unanimated, rejected as legitimate objects of desire or admiration. So, how to proceed? Douglass comes to our rescue, showing how a person of the utmost moral seriousness and intellectual integrity could move from a position of radical alienation to one of genuine attachment—and do so through a searching confrontation with the founding documents. Douglass demonstrates how grievance and gratitude can be balanced in thoughtful patriotism.

12 Years a Garrisonian

Born into slavery in Maryland in 1818, Douglass escaped bondage with a daring flight north in 1838, settling in Massachusetts. Despite his status as a runaway, subject to recapture, he soon commenced his career as an abolitionist. With the publication of his autobiography in 1845, Douglass felt compelled to flee the country altogether; his increased prominence made life in a land of bloodhounds and man stealers too risky. He returned 21 months later, after British friends secured his manumission with a payment of $711.66 (about $30,000 in today's money) to Douglass's "owner."

Not surprisingly, Douglass always viewed the United States from the perspective of the enslaved. His first impulse was to denounce the nation, root and branch. That impulse led him to become a follower of William Lloyd Garrison, who radicalized the antislavery movement with his pronouncement that the US Constitution was a "covenant with death, and an agreement with hell."[2] On the abolitionist lecture circuit, Douglass could give full-throated expression to his righteous anger. While many of today's students haven't the religious foundation or familiarity with the classics that shaped the powerful eloquence of the self-educated former slave, they would applaud his sentiments:

> How can I love a country that dooms three millions of my brethren, some of them my own kindred, my own brothers, my own sisters, who are now clanking the chains of Slavery upon the plains of the South, whose warm blood is now making fat the soil of Maryland and of Alabama, and over whose crushed spirits rolls the dark shadow of oppression, shutting out and extinguishing forever, the cheering rays of that bright sun of Liberty lighted in the souls of all God's children by the Omnipotent hand of Deity itself? How can I, I say, love a country thus cursed, thus bedewed with the blood of my brethren? A country, the Church of which, and the Government of which, and the Constitution of which, is in favour of supporting and perpetuating this monstrous system of injustice and blood? I have not, I cannot have, any love for this country, as such, or for its Constitution. I desire to see its overthrow as speedily as possible, and its Constitution shivered in a thousand fragments, rather than this foul curse should continue to remain as now.[3]

For Douglass, this verdict committed him to revolution. So long as he embraced the Garrisonian principle of "No Union with Slaveholders," Douglass called for the annulment of the Constitution and the breakup of the Union. While some students today pursue a visceral, activist anti-Americanism, most young people draw a different lesson. Their hostility to America's disgraceful past compounds their preexisting political apathy. As Alexis de Tocqueville predicted, equality of conditions can lead Americans to withdraw into narrow self-absorption.[4]

To counteract the indifference of an individualistic society, the Garrisonians relied on appeals to universal humanitarianism. The cosmopolitan outlook was explicit; the masthead of Garrison's newspaper, *The Liberator*, bore the motto "OUR COUNTRY IS THE WORLD—OUR COUNTRYMEN ARE MANKIND." Today's students are often cosmopolitans, but that stance is now mostly shorn of its Garrisonian fervor. They are disaffected cosmopolitans.

One reason why Douglass is so suited to our moment is that he was not content to remain alienated from the land of his birth. Cosmopolitanism did not satisfy him. His quest to belong can be glimpsed even in his earliest expressions of non-belonging. In a letter written to Garrison from Belfast and published in *The Liberator*, Douglass begins by asserting, "As to nation, I belong to none." He is a sojourner in the British Isles—welcomed on terms of equality and celebrated as a hero—but still an itinerant stranger. While he has "no . . . resting-place abroad," he also has "no protection at home." Significantly, Douglass calls the United States "home." Repeatedly, he calls it "the land of my birth"—from which he is an "outcast" and an "outlaw."[5] Douglass is self-reflective about his uprooted condition, which he recognizes as anomalous:

> That men should be patriotic is to me perfectly natural; and as a philosophical fact, I am able to give it an *intellectual* recognition. But no further can I go. If ever I had any patriotism, or any capacity for the feeling, it was whipt out of me long since by the lash of the American soul-drivers.[6] (Emphasis in original.)

Douglass understands his deracination as an artifact of enslavement.

Thomas Jefferson was aware of this phenomenon—and he lamented it. In the famous query 18 in *Notes on the State of Virginia*, Jefferson described a situation in which "one half the citizens" were allowed "to trample on the rights of the other." He predicted that the trampler citizens would lose their morals and be transformed into "despots," while the trampled-upon citizens would lose their "amor patriæ" and be transformed into "enemies."[7] Jefferson spoke feelingly of the slaves' dilemma:

> If a slave can have a country in this world, it must be any other in preference to that in which he is born to live and labour for another: in which he must lock up the faculties of his nature, contribute as far as depends on his individual endeavors to the evanishment of the human race, or entail his own miserable condition on the endless generations proceeding from him.[8]

Chattel slavery doesn't just steal one's labor and damage one's human potential; by extending that condition into the indefinite future, it sours the race against its own continuance. Slavery sabotages the divine injunction to "be fruitful and multiply." Attempting to rally support for gradual emancipation in Virginia, Jefferson was frank in affixing blame: "The statesman" who permitted the perpetuation of slavery should be "loaded" with "execration."[9] Douglass obliged him by denouncing "our piratical fathers."[10]

Yet immediately after declaring himself a man without a country, Douglass admits that he responds to the beauties of America's natural environment. In exile, he imagines "her bright blue sky—her grand old woods—her fertile fields—her beautiful rivers—her mighty lakes, and star-crowned mountains." But once again, he is brought up short:

> When I remember . . . that her most fertile fields drink daily of the warm blood of my outraged sisters, I am filled with unutterable loathing, and led to reproach myself that any thing could fall from my lips in praise of such a land.[11]

Douglass is doing something interesting here with the concepts of blood and soil. (Remember, he is writing a century before the repulsive Nazi version of *Blut und Boden* nationalism.) Douglass points to a kind of natural, aesthetic attachment to one's native land, as well as a natural attachment to one's blood kin. Because of slavery, these two forms of love of one's own, which normally would be mutually reinforcing, are at odds. For Douglass, the blood claim of his "sable brethren" negates his American nativity: "America," he says, "will not allow her children to love her." Yet when Douglass prays for the nation to repent at the close of this paragraph, he does so not only for the sake of the oppressed but for the sake of America itself, "before it is too late."[12]

Douglass expressed this concern more explicitly in another public letter addressed to Horace Greeley, editor of the *New-York Tribune*. Douglass's international public speaking campaign had made him more hated than ever in anti-abolition circles. The *New York Express*, a rival paper to Greeley's *Tribune*, had accused Douglass of "running a muck in greedy-eared Britain against America, its people, its institutions, and even against its peace." Since Greeley had reprinted Douglass's account of his Irish tour, Douglass, now in Scotland, ventured to communicate directly with Greeley.

Douglass begins by mentioning that this is his first attempt "to write a letter for any other than a strictly anti-slavery press." Perhaps this new audience influences his rhetoric, as he undertakes to defend himself against the charge of anti-Americanism. Expressing the "ardent hope that the curse of slavery will not much longer be permitted . . . to spread its foul mantle of moral blight, mildew and infamy, over the otherwise noble character of the American people," Douglass writes to explain why it has been necessary to expose "the sins of one nation in the ear of another."[13]

Instead of repeating that he is not and cannot be a patriot, Douglass presents his shaming of the United States as the act of a friend:

> I am one of those who think the best friend of a nation is he
> who most faithfully rebukes her for her sins—and he her worst

enemy, who, under the specious and popular garb of patriotism seeks to excuse, palliate, and defend them.[14]

At this point, patriotism remains suspect, the proverbial last refuge of
a scoundrel. Though not yet a lover of the nation, Douglass is prepared to
speak of friendship and to couch his chastisements in more sympathetic
terms. Referring to "the immortal Jefferson," Douglass echoes the Virginian's concern for the moral fiber of the nation. He declares that his aim is
"to give such an exposition of the degrading influence of slavery upon the
master and his abettors as well as upon the slave" as will "shame [America]
out of her adhesion to a system . . . at war with her own free institutions."[15]

The mention of "free institutions" signals a new attentiveness on Douglass's part to politics and the demands of persuasive speech. We should
recall how radically apolitical the Garrisonians were. Many of them were
"no government" men—pacifists and millenarian utopians. From their
perspective, slavery was just the most visible form of the violence endemic
to all human rule. Garrison and his disciples relied on divine law to con-
demn American sinfulness. Their text was the Bible, and their favored
genre of speech the jeremiad. Much of their vituperation was trained on
the US Constitution, which they interpreted as a thoroughly proslavery
compact. Although the Garrisonians certainly agreed with the Declaration's assertion that "all men are created equal," they did not attempt to
use the document as an antislavery resource, viewing it instead as a giant
fraud from the get-go. They preferred the unadulterated primary source:
the Word of God.

In Ireland, however, Douglass met abolitionists who considered themselves "the warmest friends of America and American institutions." In his
letter to Greeley, he remarks that he frequently saw the American Declaration of Independence on display in their parlors. He tells of a Dubliner
whose home featured not only the Declaration but "a number of portraits
of the distinguished founders of the American Republic." Gazing on an
expensively framed copy of the Declaration, the "aged anti-slavery gentleman" confessed that he was "often tempted to turn its face to the wall,

it is such a palpable contradiction of the spirit and practices of the American people at this time." Douglass quotes the testimony of John Quincy Adams, who feared that "the preservation, propagation and perpetuation of Slavery" had over time become "the vital and animating spirit of the American Government."[16] If the problem is the abandonment of the founding principles by subsequent generations—if it is the sons of the fathers who have turned the Declaration's face to the wall—then a better strategy might be to restore the Declaration to its original prominence. Revolution, in its literal and conservative meaning of revolving back to the starting point, could be a promising path.

Despite evincing glimmerings of another way, Douglass while abroad continued to argue not for a restored Union but for disunion. The Mexican-American War, which threatened to extend slavery's reach, demonstrated to him that even "Old Massachusetts" was "now in the piratical grasp of Texas."[17] Writing from London in August 1846 to the Anti-Slavery Sewing Circle of Lynn, Massachusetts,[18] Douglass held to the Garrisonian ultraist view that the founding was to blame. He tells the ladies:

> The deed was done long ago. The foundation of this frowning monument of infamy was laid when the States were first declared the *United States*. This is but another link around your necks of the galling chain which your fathers placed about the heels of my race. It is the legitimate fruit of compromise—of attempting a union of freedom with slavery. All was lost in that sad moment. . . . The Union must be dissolved, or New England is lost and swallowed up by the slave-power of the country.[19] (Emphasis in original.)

In his lengthy "Farewell Speech to the British People" in March 1847, Douglass continued to speak in full jeremiad mode.[20] Dropping any reference to "the otherwise noble character of the American people," he asserts that "the entire network of American society, is one great falsehood, from beginning to end."[21] Of the beginnings, Douglass says,

In their celebrated Declaration of Independence, they made the loudest and clearest assertions of the rights of man; and yet at that very time the identical men who drew up that Declaration of Independence, and framed the American democratic constitution, were trafficking in the blood and souls of their fellow men.[22]

While he has "no word of patriotic applause for America or her institutions," he is full of praise for England, where for the first time in his life he has "known what it was to enjoy liberty." It turns out that "liberty under a monarchy is better than despotism under a democracy."[23] And yet Douglass chooses to "go home." He does so, he says, "for the sake of my brethren . . . to suffer with them; to toil with them; to endure insult with them; to undergo outrage with them; . . . to speak and write in their vindication."[24] Upon his return, in May 1847, Douglass delivered his most famous statement of disaffection: "I have no love for America, as such; I have no patriotism. I have no country. What country have I? The institutions of this country do not know me, do not recognize me as a man."[25]

Five months later, in another major speech titled "American Slavery," there appeared a glimmer of a shift in Douglass's approach. As in that April 1846 letter to Greeley, Douglass explores the elements of his temperament that open him to patriotism. He possesses, he says, "all the moral material." He recurs to his attachment to the soil, which can induce in him "a sort of glow." He expresses admiration for the American character, with its "enterprise" and "industry," and takes the dramatic step of admitting that he "can read with pleasure your Constitution to establish justice, and secure the blessings of liberty to posterity." However, these "precious sayings" are invalidated when he remembers "the blood of my own blood . . . toiling under the lash." Yet immediately after reiterating that he "make[s] no pretension to patriotism,"[26] he again floats that alternative definition of patriotism that privileges dissent:

I will hold up America to the lightning scorn of moral indignation. In doing this, I shall feel myself discharging the duty of a

true patriot; for he is a lover of his country who rebukes and
does not excuse its sins.[27]

In April 1846, Douglass described himself as a friend of the nation;
now, in September 1847, he speaks of being a lover. At the same time,
since he still believes that the Constitution is "radically and essentially
slave-holding," he refuses to vote or engage in political organizing.[28] The
tools of the citizen are off-limits. As a disciple of Garrison, Douglass
rejected the abolitionist Liberty Party and others who sought reform from
within the constitutional order: "Vainly you talk about voting it down. . . .
Nothing but God's truth and love can cleanse the land. We must change
the moral sentiment."[29] For the Garrisonians, morality and politics were
irreconcilable.

Breaking Free

In launching his own abolitionist newspaper, *The North Star*, in December 1847, Douglass boldly announced, "We shall try to have a mind of
our own."[30] He more than delivered on that aspiration. Once out of the
orbit of the Garrisonians, having relocated to Rochester, New York, Douglass undertook "a reconsideration of the whole subject."[31] In the upshot,
he completely reversed his position on four key matters: disunionism,
pacifism, the nonvoting principle, and the proslavery character of the
US Constitution.

Although dramatic, this about-face was not abrupt. Douglass's change
of opinion, officially announced in May 1851, was the result of much reading, much thought, and much debate. In his autobiography, he says he
studied, "with some care, not only the just and proper rules of legal interpretation, but the origin, design, nature, rights, powers, and duties of civil
government, and also the relations which human beings sustain to it."[32]
It's not an exaggeration to say that Douglass discovered political philosophy, and it cured him of Garrisonianism and gave him his country back.

Douglass's reconsideration focused almost entirely on the Constitution. As early as February 1849, he was prepared to admit that, if strictly construed, the document was not proslavery. However, that admission meant little to him, since he did not think the letter of the law should determine interpretation. Instead, as he explained,

> the original intent and meaning of the Constitution (the one given to it by the men who framed it, those who adopted it, and the one given to it by the Supreme Court of the United States) makes it a pro-slavery instrument.[33]

This emphasis on original intent, original meaning, and, especially, the subsequent practice of the nation was characteristic of the Garrisonian approach.

In this same month, John C. Calhoun, joined by 48 Southern politicians, published an address to his fellow Southerners warning of "acts of aggression and encroachment" by an abolitionized North.[34] In response, Douglass penned a detailed and sarcastic critique of the address.[35] Calhoun and company had argued that the Constitution explicitly recognized and protected slavery. Of the language for the return of escapees, Calhoun had asserted, "All is clear. There is not an uncertain or equivocal word to be found in the whole provision."[36] In response to this misrepresentation, Douglass delights to point out that "the word slave . . . is the word of this conclave, and not of the Constitution."[37] Douglass brandishes the interpretative possibilities that unfold because of the Constitution's lack of clarity:

> The language in each of the provisions to which the address refers, though doubtless *intended* to bolster up slavery, and to respect slave property, has been so ambiguously worded as to bear a very different construction; and taken in connection with the preamble of that instrument, the very opposite of the construction given it by this wily band of slaveholders, and they have just reason to apprehend that such a construction may yet be placed

upon that instrument as shall prove the downfall of slavery.[38] (Emphasis in original.)

While Douglass sees the political advantage of constitutional literalism (if it does not say "slave," it does not mean "slave"), he is not yet prepared to adopt it. Here, he remains fixed in his view of the founders' nefarious intention. The absence of the words "slave" or "slavery" from the Constitution indicates the wicked cunning of the drafters, who "were ashamed of the *name*" of their crime but adept in devising federal protection for it.[39] (Emphasis in original.) Thus, Douglass affirms the slavocrats' brutally honest translation of the Constitution's shamefaced euphemisms:

> We are for admitting that the Constitution is just what these slaveholders in this address say it is; and on conscientious grounds demand the immediate dissolution of the American Union, as required by liberty and the law of the living God.[40]

Whether or not slaveholders took note of Douglass's journalism, abolitionists certainly did. His flirtation with literalism occasioned much excitement, with his Boston associates suspecting him of incipient apostasy, while political-action types like Gerrit Smith were greatly pleased. Douglass responded in March 1849 with another long piece, "The Constitution and Slavery," which walks a tightrope stretched above the abolitionist factions.[41] He begins by insisting that his "only aim is to know what is truth and what is duty," as a result of which he holds himself "perfectly free to change [his] opinion in any direction, and at any time which may be indicated by our immediate apprehension of truth, unbiased by the smiles or frowns of any class or party of abolitionists."[42] No such change, however, is announced, as Douglass then simply rehearses the Garrisonian take on each of the supposed slave provisions of the Constitution and repeats the standard call for "immediate disannulment."[43]

At the end of the piece, however, Douglass does take the very un-Garrisonian step of saying that he is "prepared to hear all sides" and give a "candid consideration" to the views of "our friend Gerrit Smith." Inviting Smith to write for *The North Star*, Douglass assures him that

> he cannot have a stronger wish to turn every rightful instrumentality against slavery, than we have; and if the Constitution can be so turned, and he can satisfy us of the fact, we shall readily, gladly and zealously turn our feeble energies in that direction.[44]

This truth-seeking humility on Douglass's part is crucial. Today's students could already benefit by following along as Douglass weighs the evidence and changes his mind, but maybe more important than the substantive transformation is the attitude that makes transformation possible. Douglass refuses to regard his current position on the Constitution as "correct beyond the possibility of an honest doubt."[45] By granting a hearing to those who disagree with him, he is not allowed to dismiss them as "bent upon making the worse appear the better reason."[46] Of course, there is such a thing as sophistry—Douglass was convinced that Calhoun was a sophist—but it must be proved, not assumed. One must start from the arguments rather than the ascription of motives. In 1849, Douglass pursued this more naive approach of epistemic uncertainty with respect to the Liberty Party, but it soon led him to approach the founders—and the charters they drafted—with the same open-mindedness.

"Months of Thought and Investigation"

The next two years consisted of a back-and-forth with Smith, in part by private letters, in part through public exchanges. The engagement began in earnest in March 1849, when Douglass delivered "Comments on Gerrit Smith's Address." Douglass begins by separating the "ought" from the "is." Agreeing with Smith that "government ought to be just, merciful, holy," Douglass states that the question at issue is "what the government of the United States is *authorized to be, and to do, by the Constitution of the United States.*" (Emphasis in original.) Unlike Smith, who wanted to make the law (including the Constitution itself) "subject to the understanding of right," Douglass rebuts by saying that "the Supreme Court has no conscience above the Constitution of the United States." Basically, the higher law is not constitutional law. Instead, Douglass defends the notion of a written Constitution as an essential check on "the voice of an ever-shifting majority, be that good or evil."[47]

Douglass defends constitutionalism, even if not the US Constitution. So, unless Smith can offer rules of reading that justify the importation of natural law into the written law, Douglass will

> continue to understand the Constitution not only in the light
> of its letter, but in view of its history, the meaning attached
> to it by its framers, the men who adopted it, and the circum-
> stances in which it was adopted.[48]

Douglass certainly sees the strategic advantage in Smith's antislavery reading: "We candidly confess that, could we see the Constitution as they do, we should not be slow in using the ballot-box against the system of slavery, or urging others to do so."[49] However, Douglass is not a utilitarian consequentialist: "If there is one Christian principle more firmly fixed in our heart than another, it is this, that it is wrong to do evil that good may come."[50] Douglass will not act unless he believes he has moral right, and hence moral power, on his side.

Paying more attention to the tumultuous political scene in the lead-up to the Compromise of 1850, Douglass penned harsh evaluations of "crafty" Henry Clay and "temporizing" Daniel Webster.[51] As battles over slavery broke out on many fronts, the old idea of gradual emancipation coupled with expatriation experienced a revival of sorts. Decades earlier, Jefferson had proposed this two-pronged approach when he undertook to revise the laws of Virginia in the immediate wake of the American Revolution.[52] For Jefferson, colonization offered a way to make good on the fundamental natural right to liberty of all persons without having to grant political rights and civic equality to blacks in America.[53] The American Colonization Society (ACS) had been founded in 1816 to implement this tidy "solution" to the twin dilemmas of slavery and race. The roster of supporters was impressive, including founding-era statesmen James Madison and James Monroe, as well as noted abolitionists Garrison and Smith.

However, by the 1830s, abolitionists of all stripes had abandoned the project in disgust, with Garrison penning a full exposé of the ACS's pro-slavery motives and effects in his 1832 *Thoughts on African Colonization*. Garrison devoted the entire second part of the work, "Sentiments of the People of Color," to documenting the overwhelmingly hostile reaction of free blacks to the idea of exodus. Spanning the years 1817 to 1832, 60 pages' worth of anti-colonization statements issued by gatherings of free blacks throughout the country (including in Delaware, Maryland, and Washington, DC, where slavery was legal) showed that Jefferson's prediction that oppression would erode the love of home had been wrong. Garrison concluded that "their *amor patriæ* is robust and deathless," felt even by "the unhappy slave."[54]

Despite the ambivalence we have seen from Douglass respecting patriotism, he never wavered in his opposition to emigration schemes. Indeed, his very first public speech, only six months after escaping slavery, was a denunciation of colonization. We don't have the text of his remarks, but we know that the 21-year-old runaway slave "Mr. Douglass" participated in a gathering of "colored citizens" in New Bedford, Massachusetts, on March 12, 1839. Interestingly (and unusually for these protests), the resolutions they adopted were modeled on the Declaration of Independence. After quoting the self-evident truths of equality and liberty, the document appeals to the sovereignty of the people to declare that

> when any of that people shall become honestly convinced that Slavery and African Colonization tends to tyranny, or are anti-republican in their nature, it is their *right*, it is their *duty* . . . to take a manly, a decided and an inflexible stand against the usurpation of their dearest rights.[55] (Emphasis in original.)

The signers pledge themselves

> *determined* to lay our unfettered bodies on the soil that gave us birth; and in the language of the red man to exclaim, "Shall we say to the bones of our *fathers* in yonder graves, get ye up and, go thither?"[56] (Emphasis in original.)

Assuming that the Native American reference is to the Cherokee removal and the Trail of Tears, which began in 1838, the New Bedford meeting threatens to resist—"Come weal, come woe, come life or death!"—any attempts at forced relocation. Despite the revolutionary temper of the document, it also affirms, perhaps inconsistently, that Garrison's "principles of NON-RESISTANCE are not detrimental to the abolition of American slavery."[57]

Serving as president of the ACS from 1836 to 1849 ("He is President of nothing else," said Douglass snidely), Clay was a frequent target for abolitionist criticism.[58] He was singled out in the 1839 New Bedford resolutions. In response to an 1847 speech Clay gave in Lexington, Kentucky, Douglass wrote a public letter, "To Henry Clay," wherein he accused Clay of "pretended opposition to Slavery" and "mere cant, by which to seduce the North into your support."[59] He counsels Clay, as one "in the very winter of life" who must be beyond "any ambitious desires to become the President of the United States," to

> emancipate your own slaves. . . . Leave them free as the Father of his country left his, and let your name go down to posterity, as his came down to us, a slaveholder, to be sure, but a repentant one.[60]

Still lingering on the political scene in 1849, Clay triggered a renewed "out with the negroes" movement in Kentucky in consequence of his proposal for gradual emancipation in conjunction with expatriation. Douglass responded to Kentucky's interest in federal funding for colonization with a blistering editorial, closing with the lines "We live here—have lived here—have a right to live here, and mean to live here."[61]

A strong oppositional reflex was a confirmed element in Douglass's character. His master's ban on learning to read inspired the young Douglass to master the alphabet on his own—and, in doing so, to overmaster his master. When the masters sought to solidify slavery by uprooting free blacks, Douglass thrust his American roots deeper. His speech in Boston's Faneuil Hall on May 31, 1849, set forth black claims on the continent and the nation. He points out that the black presence on the soil was contemporaneous with the European presence. Beyond the simple right to be there, blacks have claims to citizenship based on contribution ("Some of our number have fought and bled for this country") and devotion ("We are lovers of this country").[62]

The conclusion of the speech strikes a new note of militant resistance. Douglass created a sensation when he said he would welcome the news that "the slaves had risen in the South, and that the sable arms which had been engaged in beautifying and adorning the South were engaged in spreading death and devastation there." Douglass invokes the American Revolution (as well as the French Revolution of 1848), summoning Americans to be consistent in their Lockean political philosophy: "There is a state of war at the South at this moment. . . . Should you not hail, with equal pleasure, the tidings from the South that the slaves had risen . . . ?"[63] In throwing off Garrisonian nonresistance and pacifism, Douglass returned to the lessons he learned at age 16 during his physical battle against the brutal slave breaker Edward Covey: "A man without force is without the essential dignity of humanity."[64]

Once his philosophy was in accord with his natural temperament, Douglass made full use of the 1776 appeal. Witness this example from his autobiography:

> The slaveholder, kind or cruel, is a slaveholder still—the every
> hour violator of the just and inalienable rights of man; and he is,
> therefore, every hour silently whetting the knife of vengeance

for his own throat. He never lisps a syllable in commendation of the fathers of this republic, nor denounces any attempted oppression of himself, without inviting the knife to his own throat, and asserting the rights of rebellion for his own slaves.[65]

In the legislative maneuverings of 1850, Douglass was disgusted by Clay and disappointed in Webster. He was more impressed with a newcomer to the Senate, William H. Seward. Nonetheless, he found deficiencies in the scope of Seward's opposition to the compromise measures.[66] Whereas Seward demanded "the Rights of *Habeas Corpus* and Jury Trial" for suspected fugitives (an attempt to provide protection for free blacks), Douglass regarded "the trial of a man for his freedom" as an abomination, because the "right to liberty" is indefeasible for all men, runaways or not.[67] While the Garrisonians denounced slavery as sin, Douglass began to focus more on slavery as a violation of rights. The shift is subtle. Certainly, Douglass grounded his understanding of human beings as rights-bearing individuals in equal creation by God, but his language was becoming more political, less exclusively religious. As he explains in his second "Lecture on Slavery," the right to liberty "is self-evident" and

existed in the very idea of man's creation. It was *his* even before he comprehended it. He was created in it, endowed with it, and it can never be taken from him. No laws, no statutes, no compacts, no compromises, no constitutions, can abrogate or destroy it.[68] (Emphasis in original.)

In 1850, Douglass recognized that "the present storm-tossed condition of the public mind" involved not only the compromise measures themselves but the battle over the character of the Constitution.[69] In an editorial titled "Oath to Support the Constitution," Douglass formulated his rejection of the document in a new way. Instead of reasserting the proslavery character of the Constitution (on which Garrisonians and Calhounites spoke with one voice), he now argued that "Liberty and Slavery—opposite as Heaven and Hell—are both in the Constitution."[70] Douglass seems to have become more receptive to the constitutional arguments made by the Liberty Party and the new Free Soil Party, both of which highlighted the antislavery character of the Constitution.

Nonetheless, because of this "fundamental contradiction" embedded in the document, Douglass argued that an oath to support the Constitution is logically impossible for either the slaveholders or the proponents of "Free Soil" in the North. While heartened by the Free Soil members' rejection of the Compromise of 1850, Douglass was not convinced that their subscription to the Constitution could be made legitimate "based on alleged necessity."[71]

> They have a theory of human government, which makes it necessary to do evil, that good may come. We are not convinced that that theory is correct; and we must continue to hold, *for the present*, that the Constitution, being at war with itself, cannot be lived up to, and what we cannot do, we ought not to swear to do; and that, therefore, the platform for us to occupy, is outside that piece of parchment.[72] (Emphasis added.)

Note how carefully Douglass hedges his current rejectionist position with that qualifying phrase "for the present." While continuing to remain "outside" the Constitution, Douglass is more forthright in asserting his patriotism. The crisis of 1850 had brought forth much talk of patriotism as partisans made the case for various Union-saving measures. In a series of seven lectures on "American Slavery" begun in December 1850, Douglass was willing to bid for the label. Contrasting his "genuine patriotism" with the version "impiously" arrayed on the side of slavery, Douglass said, "I, too, would invoke the spirit of patriotism."[73]

In a private letter to Smith in January 1851, Douglass indicated his frustration with the perversity of the Garrisonian position: "I have about decided to let Slaveholders and their Northern abettors have the Laboring *oar* in putting a proslavery interpretation upon the Constitution. I am sick and tired of arguing on the slaveholders' side of this question."[74] (Emphasis in original.) The sticking point for Douglass remained his understanding of the "intentions of the framers."[75] He was prepared to admit that a sole focus on the text may be a sound hermeneutic for legal documents, but he had lingering moral qualms. The passage is worth quoting in full:

> May we avail ourselves of legal rules which enable us to defeat even the wicked intentions of our Constitution makers? It is this question which puzzles me more than all others involved in the subject. Is it good morality to take advantage of a legal flaw and put a meaning upon a legal instrument the very opposite of what we have good reason to believe was the intention of the men who framed it? Just here is the question of difficulty with me. I know well enough that slavery is an outrage, contrary to all ideas of justice, and therefore cannot be law according to Blackstone. But may it not be law according to American legal authority?[76]

Less than four months later, in another letter to Smith, Douglass had resolved his qualms. Referring to "months of thought and investigation," he announced that he was "prepared to contend for those rules of interpretation which when applied to the Constitution make its details harmonize with its declared objects in its preamble."[77] Three weeks later, he issued the forthright editorial "Change of Opinion Announced."[78] Over the next decade, he would detail how he read the various contested clauses of the Constitution, but here he limited himself to highlighting the disadvantage of his previous mode of interpretation:

> We found, in our former position, that, when debating the question, we were compelled to go behind the letter of the Constitution, and to seek its meaning in the history and practice of the nation under it—a process always attended with disadvantages; and certainly we feel little inclination to shoulder disadvantages of any kind, in order to give slavery the slightest protection.[79]

Demanding that the Constitution "be wielded in behalf of emancipation," Douglass now regarded both the charter of government and its ordinary processes, especially the ballot, as "powerful instrumentalities against Slavery."[80]

"Cling to This Day—Cling to It, and to Its Principles"

What enabled Douglass to finally reconcile morality with politics? Certainly, the results are clear: The reconciliation made him pro-Union (now arguing that slavery would be abolished only through the Union rather than through its dismemberment), pro–political party (now faced with difficult decisions about whether to support only Liberty Party candidates or more moderate Free Soil and eventually Republican candidates), and pro–slave insurrection (hence his endorsement of resistance to the Fugitive Slave Act and his financial support for John Brown). Never does Douglass say he switched to a Machiavellian calculus that one can do evil to produce good—although, of course, Machiavellians usually don't own their "effectual truth." My view is that Douglass continued a man of principle; he did not give up on doing rightly, but he did add the virtue of political prudence to his understanding of a principled life. Prudence permits one to choose the lesser of two evils. Let's say Douglass moved from Immanuel Kant not all the way to Machiavelli but to the proper mean of Aristotle.

There is one clue about the final stage of Douglass's conversion. Unlike some of his new mentors, especially Lysander Spooner, dean of the antislavery constitutionalists, Douglass did not "fling to the winds" the question of authorial intention.[81] With his "*sola scriptura*" rule of interpretation, Spooner had disallowed "all speculations as to the opinions of the Constitution makers."[82] In another letter to Smith, Douglass says something a little different: "I am only in reason and in conscience bound to learn the intentions of those who framed the Constitution *in the Constitution itself.*"[83] (Emphasis in original.) For Douglass, intention still matters and is discoverable in the text. The text is the record of its maker's intention—an intention that can then be confirmed through knowledge of the historical record.

Over the course of the 1850s, Douglass's interest in the founders grew as he developed a sophisticated reading of the text that did not scorn research into the wider context. In a certain sense, both the extreme Garrisonian proslavery reading and the extreme Spoonerian antislavery reading were the creations of purists. As soon as Garrison espied compromise in a document (or an institution or a person), he rejected it as hopelessly compromised. Spooner, too, was an absolutist of sorts. He simply refused to see any compromise with slavery in the Constitution. The charter was worthy of support because it was pure, with the admirable preamble controlling the meaning of each provision and invalidating any interpretation at odds with true justice. Yet for most Americans—who did know something of their history—Spooner's literalism seemed too much like a semantic trick. It's true that the words "slave" and "slavery" do not appear in the Constitution. But is slavery there all the same? And if so, what does that mean about our ability to swear an oath to the Constitution?

What Douglass achieved was a vindication of the founders' intent. Instead of denying the presence of compromises in the document, he reexamined key provisions to see whether they amounted to a compromise of the principle of human liberty. Is it possible to construct a compromise that isn't compromising? The paradox here is a permanent one. Should we celebrate the spirit of compromise and mutual concession? Should we venerate those statesmen who ingeniously craft modes of adjustment that pacify intestine feuds? Should we lament the rise of extremists for whom "compromise" is a dirty word?

Yes, yes, and yes. And yet "compromise" is sometimes a dirty word: "She compromised herself and all she ever stood for" or "they were discovered in a compromising position." Garrison was always uncompromising, but the supremely prudent Abraham Lincoln could also be uncompromising. Think of the intransigence on display in the final paragraph of Lincoln's 1860 Cooper Union address:

Neither let us be slandered from our duty by false accusations against us, nor frightened from it by menaces of destruction to the Government nor of dungeons to ourselves. let us have faith that right makes might, and in that faith, let us, to the end, dare to do our duty as we understand it.[84]

As Douglass's experience of the world grew, he became more discerning in his evaluations of the proper types of, and times for, compromise. He never joined in the admiration for Clay, "the Great Pacificator" who engineered both the Missouri Compromise and the Compromise of 1850, but he did come to value the "prudence" spoken of in the Declaration and the principle-preserving, practical compromises devised by the antislavery delegates to the Constitutional Convention.[85]

To illustrate, take Douglass's verdict on the Constitution's much-maligned three-fifths clause. Unlike Spooner, Douglass is willing to concede that "all other Persons" does refer to the enslaved population. Of course, from a consistently antislavery perspective, it would have been preferable not to count the enslaved at all, since counting them either fully or fractionally increased the slaveholding states' political power in both the House of Representatives and the Electoral College.

Yet in Douglass's view, even as a compromise measure, the three-fifths clause "leans to freedom."[86] How so? Douglass points out that it deprived the slaveholding states of two-fifths of the enslaved portion of "their natural basis of representation"—that natural basis being simply all the men, women, and children of a region.[87] Thus, the provision can be understood as a penalty levied on those states that persisted in denying liberty to their population. Granting that it was not in the Constitutional Convention's power to place all human beings on a footing of equal liberty, the document can be admired for the way in which it "leans to freedom." In the midst of widespread unfreedom, the Constitution presses in the better direction.

What about the Constitution's avoidance of the words "slave" and "slavery"? Whereas the Garrisonians denounced the resort to euphemism as a connivance, Douglass saw that it could instead be seen as an antislavery success since the refusal to use those words denied any constitutional legitimacy to "property in man."[88] Slavery existed under the laws of the separate states, but it did not exist under, by, or through the Constitution of the United States. We might say the founders built better than they lived, in hopes that the building could serve as a permanent dwelling for a post-slavery nation. In his further study of the founding era, Douglass found plenty of evidence that in the decades before the invention of the cotton gin, "all regarded slavery as an expiring and doomed system, destined to speedily disappear from the country."[89] This insight allowed Douglass to see the flaw in the Garrisonian tendency to judge the past based on the present, attributing the obvious vices of mid-19th-century America to the original plan. Employing his knack for metaphor, Douglass stated:

> The American Government and the American Constitution . . . are as distinct in character as is a ship and a compass. The one may point right and the other steer wrong. A chart is one thing, the course of the vessel is another. The Constitution may be right, the Government wrong. If the Government has been governed by mean, sordid, and wicked passions, it does not follow that the Constitution is mean, sordid, and wicked.[90]

The result of Douglass's comprehensive realignment can be seen in the first great speech that he delivered after his 1851 change of opinion. In the most quoted passages of "What to the Slave Is the Fourth of July?," Douglass savages the government, church, and society of the day with all his usual force. What is new and important is that this scathing denunciation is sandwiched between two sections that celebrate the nation's founding charters. Douglass begins the speech with praise for the Declaration and ends it with praise for the Constitution. Moreover, for the first time, he addresses his audience as "Fellow Citizens."[91] Throughout the 1850s, Douglass continued to defend and explicate the antislavery intention of the Constitution, defending the framers against "a slander upon their memory";[92] the July 4 address, however, stands as his most extensive tribute to the American Revolution. Above all, Douglass credits the "saving principles" of the Declaration.[93] Of the "statesmen, patriots and heroes" who contended for those principles, Douglass insists that their fight was not for themselves alone: "Their statesmanship looked beyond the passing moment, and stretched away in strength into the distant future."[94]

It is worth noting that Douglass characterizes the Revolutionary generation as having "declared for liberty."[95] Repeatedly, Douglass invokes liberty, never mentioning equality, although he does twice add "justice," referring to "the great principles of justice and freedom" and "the great principles of political freedom and of natural justice."[96] This might well strike us as surprising. Our tendency is the same as that of our students: We see slavery as a violation of the Declaration's equality principle. And, of course, it is.

Nonetheless, I think Douglass's focus on liberty is the more natural and sound approach.[97] The real objection to enslavement is not that it treats other persons or groups unequally but that it deprives the enslaved of their liberty. After all, one could remedy the inequality by enslaving everyone (a possibility in degenerate democracy about which Tocqueville warned). What mattered to Douglass was the moral content of equality. Was there equality of rights, equality of liberty? Douglass's autobiography was titled *My Bondage and My Freedom*. Keeping that opposition in mind is an important corrective for us today, when the notion of equality has gone off the straight and narrow rails laid out by the individual natural rights to life and liberty.

A Thought for Our Time

Douglass's remarkable journey did not cease when he became physically free from enslavement. He sought fuller forms of freedom, especially political freedom. Before he could agitate for citizenship and civil rights, Douglass had to discover himself to be a political being: He found a way to belong to a political community, he became a patriot, he came to regard whites (even those who declined his fellowship) as fellow citizens, and he developed the virtues required of citizens, learning to listen as well as to speak.

Something like Douglass's roundabout journey back to 1776 must be taken by students today, who often begin from a place of political alienation. Douglass's quest was long and arduous, involving not only rigorous thought but a sentimental education of sorts. What is the lesson for teachers? Well, we can't just inform students that they have been bamboozled by ideologues and bad history. We can, however, strive to interest students in great lives and original texts. It is often better to begin not in 1776 but instead with a figure like Douglass who is still admired and who expressed reservations about the founding that resonate today. By following along with Douglass, students encounter the evidence, which turns out to be overwhelming, that the founding generation regarded all human beings, male and female, black and white, as endowed with natural rights.

Once students see that the founders might have meant what they said, then they can start to grapple with the political complexities of the era. They acquire a sense of history. They learn something of political prudence and the difference between the best and the achievable. They learn to balance appreciation and criticism. As their powers of judgment develop, they experience a dramatic release from their prejudices and a release from the sense of shame about their nation's origins that has been instilled in them. They start to wonder what else they might be misinformed about. Now they are truly students: curious, aware of important questions (both timeless ones like the ambiguity of compromise and time-bound ones like the specific compromises of the Constitution), and eager to grapple with challenging texts. They become both humble and bold. They exchange their easy moralism and their easy cynicism for something more difficult and rewarding. With any luck, they end up where Douglass did, advising his July 4 audience to "cling to this day—cling to it, and to its principles, with the grasp of a storm-tossed mariner to a spar at midnight."[98]

Notes

1. Frederick Douglass, "The Meaning of July Fourth for the Negro," in *The Life and Writings of Frederick Douglass*, ed. Philip S. Foner, vol. 2, *Pre–Civil War Decade: 1850–1860* (International Publishers, 1950), 183.

2. See *Eighth Annual Report of the Board of Managers of the Mass. Anti-Slavery Society* (Boston, 1840), 94. Garrison began publishing the abolitionist newspaper *The Liberator* in 1831 and founded the American Anti-Slavery Society in 1833.

3. Frederick Douglass, "The Right to Criticize American Institutions," speech, American Anti-Slavery Society, New York, May 11, 1847, in *The Life and Writings of Frederick Douglass*, vol. 1, *Early Years, 1817–1849* (International Publishers, 1950), 236.

4. An illustrative but mortifying example from my own classroom: a student caught shoe shopping online during a class devoted to Jefferson's fears of a postrevolutionary descent into consumerism.

5. Frederick Douglass to William Lloyd Garrison, January 1, 1846, in *The Life and Writings of Frederick Douglass*, 1:126.

6. Douglass to Garrison.

7. Thomas Jefferson, "Manners," query 18 in *Notes on the State of Virginia*, in *The Portable Thomas Jefferson*, ed. Merrill D. Peterson (Penguin Books, 1977), 214–15.

8. Jefferson, "Manners," 215.

9. Jefferson, "Manners," 214.

10. Frederick Douglass, "Comments on Gerrit Smith's Address," in *The Life and Writings of Frederick Douglass*, 1:375.

11. Douglass to Garrison.

12. Douglass to Garrison.

13. Frederick Douglass to Horace Greeley, April 15, 1846, in *The Life and Writings of Frederick Douglass*, 1:144–47. It is unclear whether the letter gained editorial favor. In Douglass's collected works, this letter shows as having been published in *The Liberator*, not the *Tribune*.

14. Douglass to Greeley, 1:161.

15. Douglass to Greeley, 1:144–49.

16. Douglass to Greeley, 1:148.

17. Frederick Douglass to William A. White, July 30, 1846, in *The Life and Writings of Frederick Douglass*, 1:182.

18. To raise money for the cause, abolitionist-minded women created items decorated with antislavery emblems, such as the Wedgwood medallion "Am I Not a Man and a Brother?"

19. Frederick Douglass to Lynn Anti-Slavery Sewing Circle, August 18, 1846, in *The Life and Writings of Frederick Douglass*, 1:187–88.

20. Frederick Douglass, "Farewell Speech to the British People," speech, London, March 30, 1847, in *The Life and Writings of Frederick Douglass*, 1:206–33.

21. Douglass, "Farewell Speech to the British People," 1:207.

22. Douglass, "Farewell Speech to the British People."

23. Douglass, "Farewell Speech to the British People," 1:229.

24. Douglass, "Farewell Speech to the British People," 1:232.

25. Douglass, "The Right to Criticize American Institutions," 1:236.

26. Frederick Douglass, "American Slavery," speech, Syracuse, NY, September 24, 1847, in *The Life and Writings of Frederick Douglass*, 1:275–76.

27. Douglass, "American Slavery," 1:276.

28. Douglass, "American Slavery," 1:274.

29. Douglass, "American Slavery," 1:278.

30. Frederick Douglass, "To Our Oppressed Countrymen," in *The Life and Writings of Frederick Douglass*, 1:282–83.

31. Frederick Douglass, *My Bondage and My Freedom*, in *Douglass: Autobiographies*, ed. Henry Louis Gates Jr. (Literary Classics of the United States, 1994), 391.

32. Douglass, *My Bondage and My Freedom*, 392.

33. Frederick Douglass to C. H. Chase, February 9, 1849, in *The Life and Writings of Frederick Douglass*, 1:353–54.

34. John C. Calhoun, "The Address of Southern Delegates in Congress to Their Constituents," *The Charleston Courier*, February 1, 1849, http://civilwarcauses.org/address.htm.

35. Frederick Douglass, "The Address of Southern Delegates in Congress to Their Constituents; or, the Address of John C. Calhoun and Forty Other Thieves," in *The Life and Writings of Frederick Douglass*, 1:353–60.

36. Calhoun, "The Address of Southern Delegates in Congress to Their Constituents."

37. Douglass, "The Address of Southern Delegates in Congress to Their Constituents," 1:355.

38. Douglass, "The Address of Southern Delegates in Congress to Their Constituents."

39. Douglass, "The Address of Southern Delegates in Congress to Their Constituents," 1:356.

40. Douglass, "The Address of Southern Delegates in Congress to Their Constituents," 1:355.

41. Frederick Douglass, "The Constitution and Slavery," in *The Life and Writings of Frederick Douglass*, 1:361–67.

42. Douglass, "The Constitution and Slavery," 1:361.

43. Douglass, "The Constitution and Slavery," 1:366.

44. Douglass, "The Constitution and Slavery."

45. Douglass, "The Constitution and Slavery."

46. Douglass, "The Constitution and Slavery."

47. Douglass, "Comments on Gerrit Smith's Address," 1:374–79.

48. Douglass, "Comments on Gerrit Smith's Address," 1:377.

49. Douglass, "Comments on Gerrit Smith's Address," 1:379.

50. Douglass, "Comments on Gerrit Smith's Address," 1:378.

51. Frederick Douglass, "Henry Clay and Slavery," in *The Life and Writings of Frederick Douglass*, 2:105–9; and Frederick Douglass, "Weekly Review of Congress," in *The Life and Writings of Frederick Douglass*, 2:109–15.

52. See Virginia General Assembly, *Report of the Committee of Revisors Appointed by the General Assembly of Virginia in MDCCLXXVI* (Richmond, VA, 1779). For Jefferson's summary and justification of the plan, see Thomas Jefferson, "Laws," query 14 in *Notes on the State of Virginia*, 185.

53. Jefferson was influenced by his belief that a biracial society of former masters and former slaves was impossible and his doubts about black intellectual capacities.

54. William Lloyd Garrison, *Thoughts on African Colonization* [. . .] (Boston, 1832).

55. *The Liberator*, "Great Anti-Colonization Meeting in New-Bedford," March 29, 1839, https://fair-use.org/the-liberator/1839/03/29/the-liberator-09-13.pdf.

56. *The Liberator*, "Great Anti-Colonization Meeting in New-Bedford."

57. *The Liberator*, "Great Anti-Colonization Meeting in New-Bedford."

58. Frederick Douglass, "The American Colonization Society," speech, Faneuil Hall, Boston, May 31, 1849, in *The Life and Writings of Frederick Douglass*, 1:387–99.

59. Frederick Douglass, "To Henry Clay," in *The Life and Writings of Frederick Douglass*, 1:284–90. Newly elected to the House of Representatives and on his way east, Lincoln was in attendance at this speech by the man he termed his "beau ideal of a statesman" and in whom Douglass saw "so much of Satan dressed in the livery of Heaven." Abraham Lincoln, "Eulogy on Henry Clay," Springfield, IL, July 6, 1852, https://www.abrahamlincolnonline.org/lincoln/speeches/clay.htm; and Douglass, "To Henry Clay," 1:289. Lincoln's and Douglass's contrary assessments of Clay (and, one might add, Brown) are food for thought.

60. Douglass, "To Henry Clay," 1:290.

61. Frederick Douglass, "Colonization," in *The Life and Writings of Frederick Douglass*, 2:352.

62. Douglass, "The American Colonization Society."

63. Douglass, "The American Colonization Society," 1:399.

64. Douglass, *My Bondage and My Freedom*, 591.

65. Douglass, *My Bondage and My Freedom*, 301–2.

66. Douglass, "Oath to Support the Constitution," in *The Life and Writings of Frederick Douglass*, 2:115–19.

67. Douglass, "Oath to Support the Constitution," 2:117, 140.

68. Frederick Douglass, "Lecture on Slavery, No. 2," lecture, Corinthian Hall, Rochester, NY, December 8, 1850, in *The Life and Writings of Frederick Douglass*, 2:140.

69. Douglass, "Oath to Support the Constitution," 2:118.

70. Douglass, "Oath to Support the Constitution."

71. Douglass, "Oath to Support the Constitution," 2:119.

72. Douglass, "Oath to Support the Constitution."

73. Douglass, "Lecture on Slavery, No. 2," 2:148.

74. Frederick Douglass to Gerrit Smith, January 21, 1851, in *The Life and Writings of Frederick Douglass*, 2:149.

75. Douglass to Smith, January 21, 1851.

76. Douglass to Smith, January 21, 1851, 2:150.

77. Frederick Douglass to Gerrit Smith, May 1, 1851, in *The Life and Writings of Frederick Douglass*, 2:152–53.

78. Frederick Douglass, "Change of Opinion Announced," in *The Life and Writings of Frederick Douglass*, 2:155–56.

79. Douglass, "Change of Opinion Announced," 1:156.

80. Douglass, "Change of Opinion Announced"; and Frederick Douglass to Gerrit Smith, April 15, 1852, Frederick Douglass Papers, https://frederickdouglasspapersproject.com/s/digitaledition/item/5600.

81. This is what Douglass says Smith does. The description is accurate with respect to Spooner as well. Douglass to Smith, January 21, 1851, 2:150.

82. Douglass to Smith, January 21, 1851. So, for instance, insight into the choices made by the Constitutional Convention could not be sought through study of the *Notes of Debates in the Federal Convention of 1787 Reported by James Madison*, first published in 1840.

83. Frederick Douglass to Gerrit Smith, May 21, 1851, in *The Life and Writings of Frederick Douglass*, 2:157.

84. Abraham Lincoln, "Address at Cooper Institute, New York City," speech, Cooper Institute, New York, February 27, 1860, in *The Collected Works of Abraham Lincoln*, ed. Roy P. Basler, vol. 3, *1858–1860* (Rutgers University Press, 1953), 550.

85. For Douglass's final assessment of the troublesome clauses of the Constitution, see Frederick Douglass, "The Constitution of the United States: Is It Pro-Slavery or Anti-Slavery?" (speech, Glasgow, Scotland, March 26, 1860), in *The Life and Writings of Frederick Douglass*, 2:467–80.

86. Douglass, "The Constitution of the United States," 2:472.

87. Douglass, "The Constitution of the United States."

88. Douglass, "The Constitution of the United States," 2:471.

89. Douglass, "The Constitution of the United States," 2:473.

90. Douglass, "The Constitution of the United States," 2:467.

91. Frederick Douglass, "The Meaning of July Fourth for the Negro," in *The Life and Writings of Frederick Douglass*, 2:181–204.

92. Douglass, "The Meaning of July Fourth for the Negro," 2:201.

93. Douglass, "The Meaning of July Fourth for the Negro," 2:185.

94. Douglass, "The Meaning of July Fourth for the Negro," 2:186–87.

95. Douglass, "The Meaning of July Fourth for the Negro," 2:186.

96. Douglass, "The Meaning of July Fourth for the Negro," 2:187–88.

97. Interestingly, Douglass does talk about equality whenever he discusses the phenomenon of "prejudice against color." He points out that the term is not accurate, since whites have no objection to proximity to blacks so long as blacks are in a

subordinate role. The objection is to the "colored gentleman." Thus, what is called color prejudice is "no less than a *murderous, hell-born hatred* of every virtue which may adorn the character of a *black man*." (Emphasis in original.) To overcome prejudice, the "doctrine of human equality" must be established. Here is how Douglass defines that doctrine: "We believe in human equality; that character, not color, should be the criterion by which to choose associates; and we pity the pride of the poor pale dust and ashes which would erect any other standard of social fellowship." Clearly, equality properly understood does not threaten discriminations based on virtue. Frederick Douglass, "Prejudice Against Color," in *The Life and Writings of Frederick Douglass*, 1:127–30.

98. Douglass, "The Meaning of July Fourth for the Negro," 2:185.

About the Authors

Randy E. Barnett is the Patrick Hotung Professor of Constitutional Law at the Georgetown University Law Center and faculty director of the Georgetown Center for the Constitution. He coauthored *The Original Meaning of the Fourteenth Amendment: Its Letter and Spirit* (2021).

Justin Driver is the Robert R. Slaughter Professor of Law at Yale Law School and the author of, among other books, *The Schoolhouse Gate: Public Education, the Supreme Court, and the Battle for the American Mind* (2018).

Kurt T. Lash is the E. Claiborne Robins Distinguished Professor of Law at the University of Richmond and the founder and director of the Richmond Program on the American Constitution. He is the author of, among numerous other books, *The Fourteenth Amendment and the Privileges or Immunities of American Citizenship* (2014).

Lucas E. Morel is the John K. Boardman, Jr., Professor of Politics at Washington and Lee University. He is the author of *Lincoln and the American Founding* (2020), among other books, and is a member of the US Semiquincentennial Commission.

Diana Schaub is professor emerita of political science at Loyola University Maryland and a nonresident senior fellow at the American Enterprise Institute. She is a visiting professor at the School of Civic Leadership at the University of Texas at Austin. Her latest book is *His Greatest Speeches: How Lincoln Moved the Nation* (2021).

About the Editors

Yuval Levin is the director of Social, Cultural, and Constitutional Studies at the American Enterprise Institute, where he also holds the Beth and Ravenel Curry Chair in Public Policy. The founder and editor of *National Affairs*, he is also a senior editor at *The New Atlantis*, a contributing editor at *National Review*, and a contributing opinion writer at *The New York Times*.

Adam J. White is the Laurence H. Silberman Chair in Constitutional Governance and a senior fellow at the American Enterprise Institute, where he focuses on the Supreme Court and the administrative state. Concurrently, he codirects the Antonin Scalia Law School's C. Boyden Gray Center for the Study of the Administrative State.

John Yoo is a nonresident senior fellow at the American Enterprise Institute; the Emanuel S. Heller Professor of Law at the University of California, Berkeley; and a senior research fellow at the Civitas Institute at the University of Texas at Austin.